With gratitude
and grace —

Kerry

D1270061

Memories of the Heart

A Story of Love, Loss, *and* Learning to Live Again

KERRY ALDRIDGE, RN

LifeRich
PUBLISHING

LifeRich Publishing is a registered trademark of
The Reader's Digest Association, Inc.

LifeRich Publishing books may be ordered through booksellers or by contacting:

LifeRich Publishing
1663 Liberty Drive
Bloomington, IN 47403
www.liferichpublishing.com
1 (888) 238-8637

Because of the dynamic nature of the Internet, any web addresses or
links contained in this book may have changed since publication and
may no longer be valid. The views expressed in this work are solely those
of the author and do not necessarily reflect the views of the publisher,
and the publisher hereby disclaims any responsibility for them.

Any people depicted in stock imagery provided by Thinkstock are models,
and such images are being used for illustrative purposes only.
Certain stock imagery © Thinkstock.

ISBN: 978-1-4897-0679-9 (sc)
ISBN: 978-1-4897-0680-5 (hc)
ISBN: 978-1-4897-0681-2 (e)

Library of Congress Control Number: 2016902357

Print information available on the last page.

LifeRich Publishing rev. date: 02/12/2016

For Jack

A great man who lived his life with gratitude and grace.

Preface

This book came about as a result of my experience of being a hospice nurse and then having to be on the other side of it when my husband Jack was dying of lung cancer. I had to learn how to not be the nurse and to be the wife. It was difficult.

I have learned a great deal first hand of what hospice patients and their families go through once they get that diagnosis. I thought I knew what they felt, but I really had no idea until I had to face it myself. Yes, I have had losses in my life, great losses, but I now realize that not having grieved those losses as well as I probably could have only compounded my grief when Jack died.

I have learned a lot, not only from my patients, but from my own experience that I would like to share with you in some small way. I have felt the emotions and the unspeakable pain that goes with living with cancer, or any other life limiting illness.

There were many people who saw me through this fourteen year struggle with Jack's cancer. I would not have been able to do it on my own. To the people who have crossed my path, and those that I have learned so much from and leaned on often, I thank you. Candy & Doug

Hawks, thank you for bringing four little grandchildren across the country, more than once to see Grandpa Jack. Your support meant more than I can say. To Jack's children, Skip & Diane Aldridge, Shari & Jerry Ronny, Susan & Paul Britton, Debbie McPhee and their families, to whom I cannot thank enough for the support and encouragement and time you gave both of us. His grandchildren gave him the reasons to fight long and hard; and he did.

JoAnn Reilly, thank you for reading this manuscript as I wrote it. It was an honor for me that you did that. Reverend Tom Madden, who supported us from day one, and after. Robert Chwast, PhD,who worked with me on anticipatory grief. David Ackerman, LISW-S, MSSA, who was there no matter the hour. Patty O'Shea, LISW, who showed me how to deal with the Dark Night of the Soul with her gracefulness and knowledge of Bereavement. My friend, Renie Blakemore,who was with me for every surgery, call, chemo, labs, etc. We could not have done it without you. And to Kathy Anne Roberts, my Twin, who literally put her life on hold, and moved across the country to help me take care of Jack. I cannot thank you enough. And last but not least, to Tom Hyman, Author and mentor at Long Ridge Writer's Group in CT, who inspired me to keep writing.

With gratitude and grace I sincerely thank you all.

Kerry

*"There are many ways of moving forward
but only one way of standing still."*

— *Franklin D. Roosevelt*

Introduction

"*G*ratitude is a memory of the heart" Rudy Sullivant once said; and he was right. It matters not if someone you lost has been gone a short time or a long time. Maybe what you are dealing with right now is living with someone you love who has a life limiting illness. Maybe what you are *living* with is the loss of that important person who was in your life. It may or may not have been a recent loss; but maybe now is the time you are ready to try to look at some small piece of it and try to heal a little bit inside. What matters is that whether they are gone or not, possibly you need a little help getting through some pieces of it that you are struggling with. It happens. We all struggle sometimes, it's normal. It can be difficult to have gratitude while you're grieving. I did struggle and sometimes I still do.

This is the story of how my late husband Jack, the love of my life, and I got through our fourteen year battle with his lung cancer one day at a time with gratitude and grace. I cannot say it was easy; it was not. Yes, there were certainly better days than others, and we were blessed with many of them, some of which I will share with you.

We had many beautiful things to be grateful for.

Some days those things were easy to find. Other days we struggled to search for them, but we found them. We had to. Life is not all sunshine and roses when you are faced with a life limiting disease or a sudden death. I trust that our story will help you find some hope and encouragement to get through whatever situation you find yourself struggling with.

Don't be offended by the humor you may run across in some pages of this book. Cancer is not funny, but Jack was. He had the best sense of humor of anyone I had ever met. He was funny long before he had cancer, and was funny long after! Cancer did not change that. He loved life and he loved to laugh and he made me laugh; a lot. So you will find humor intertwined in the pages of our story because that's who we were together, and with our friends. He could make me laugh when I was in the middle of an emotional meltdown, which occurred more often than I would like to admit. I'm really not quite sure how he did that, but he did, and I loved him for it.

There are things I struggled with many years after my Dad's death when I was a teenager and my brother's suicide when I was in my thirties. Now more recently the death of my husband just a few short years ago. There were many things, some of which I will share in this book, which we struggled with during the fourteen years that we battled with his lung cancer. Yes, I say that *we* both battled it. He physically, and both of us emotionally. It affected both our lives, and in turn our family's lives as well.

With tremendous love comes tremendous loss. I write this book with a sound mind yet a broken heart. Loss is never easy no matter the circumstance. Whatever your experience has been, or currently is, you will survive this. How *well* you do will be up to you. You will have choices, and plenty of them, to make. Some will be difficult, some easy and some will just simply be made for you by circumstance. Just as there are plenty of choices you will have to make, there are plenty of ways of going forward. There is *no* wrong way. I cannot stress this enough. This is not your friends journey, your sisters or your brothers, your cousins or your mother's. It is yours and yours individually.

There is no right or wrong when it comes to grief. Grief is as unique as the person experiencing it. What you feel, and how and when you feel it will be right for you, regardless of how someone you know may have experienced it before you. I trust you will find comfort in some of the pages of this book. Maybe after having read it you will be glad to know you are not alone. I believe that the more we understand something the less we have to fear it.

With gratitude and grace -

Kerry

"Jack"

*L*et me take a moment and introduce you to Jack. He had been called Jack his entire life, until he joined the navy and they made him go by his legal name, John. When I met him, he was introduced to me as John, and then he told me his nickname had been Jack throughout his life. Well, I liked it, so I just started calling him Jack. There were people he worked with that knew him as John and friends and others who called him Jack. He always answered to both.

I first met Jack in a class of about thirty people interested to learn about the beliefs of Bay Presbyterian Church in Bay Village, Ohio. My four –year-old twins at the time, Candy and Ryan, convinced me that we should go there because they liked the children's sermon at the beginning of the service. I had taken them there one Sunday to hear my friend Paula and her husband Glenn sing. The twins couldn't stop talking about it. I finally gave in. So I went to the class, and Jack was there. He remembered me, but I can't say I remembered him! I did remember working on a few church projects with him such as the Christmas Angel Tree, the Christmas Care Bears, and Christmas Shoe Boxes, but that's about it. He was a nice guy.

I had joined the Contemporary Gospel Choir, Promise, and we sang just about every week for the service. It was almost four years later when Jack asked me out. I was a bit surprised. I really didn't know him.

"Aren't you married?" I nervously laughed with a questioning look on my face - a look that required an answer.

"What? Married? I haven't been married for years! You keep ignoring me" he said as he smiled. I noticed he had a great smile.

"I'm not ignoring you. I thought you were married."

"I've been trying to talk to you for four years! You love football and meatball sandwiches."

"How do you know that?" Now I was beginning to wonder about this guy!

"You said it in that class we were in four years ago."

"What class?" I had no idea what he was talking about. I had forgotten about it.

"The class about what the church believes. Remember? We joined the church together on the same day!" I was embarrassed. No, I did not remember that. I had no clue as to who he was.

"You remembered that? For four years? You remembered that I love football and meatball sandwiches?!" He jogged my memory, and then I remembered saying it during the icebreaker session.

"Yep! And I have watched you sing every Sunday morning. I come here every Sunday just to watch you sing and of course listen to the sermon. And you ignore me at coffee hour ."

He smiled the biggest smile I've ever seen. He smiled a lot! He had a great smile. People would often ask me, "Does this guy always smile?" And I would say, "Always!"

He had me. I remember thinking to myself that a

man like that couldn't be all bad! After all, who really remembers what anyone says the first time they meet them? Well, he did. I married that guy from church a year later! Our friends have always laughed with us about this story and I was asked a lot, "Didn't you ever look for a ring?" No, I guess I didn't. I never thought about it. I wasn't looking for anyone. Why would I be looking for a ring? He certainly pursued me, and I am truly grateful he did.

The twenty-six years we were married felt like a blink of an eye. Clearly not long enough for either of us. I would take another twenty-six years in a heartbeat if I could. I cannot, nor can you, so I trust we will at least try to hold onto the best memories held safely tucked away in the special chambers of our hearts. We can, and will, treasure them as well as we can and for as long as we can and that will be enough. It must be enough, otherwise we can drive ourselves crazy with the 'what if's of life.

What if I had one more day, one more week, one more month, or even one more year with Jack? I have asked myself that question several times over the past few years. Would I have done anything differently? Not really. In my case I had fourteen years of what is call anticipatory grief to deal with. I knew I would have *some* kind of time - how much time, I did not know. I never in a million years dreamed it would be fourteen years, and I thanked God almost every day for those years. I say almost because to be sure there were days I wasn't talking to God, and he knew why. I was angry, very angry. There were days I was grateful, grateful that Jack was still alive. He was a train wreck at times but alive. Somehow his doctors managed to put him back together again like Humpty Dumpty after he had fallen off the wall! Yes, he had his scars and breaks and bruises, but he was put back together again as well as anyone could have been, given the situation.

Jack never complained. He knew what he had to do, and he did it. I can't say I understood at times *why* he would put himself and his body through so much, with such consequences and pain, but he did. He had his reasons, and this was his journey not mine. He never wavered in his faith. There were times that I certainly did. I felt the hand of God was heavy; Jack did not. What Jack felt was that he was a burden to the people around him, the people who loved him and were caring for him. It was hard for him to understand that he was not a burden at all. We loved him. His children and grandchildren and a lot of friends loved him. They wanted to help take care of him, and they did. I believe he eventually understood that, but it was hard for him because he was such an independent man. He was always the one giving, not receiving. It was very difficult for him to receive the help when he needed it.

Jack had a sense of humor that made life easier for everyone around him. He had such a way of making you laugh. Even when things got rough, and they got really rough at times, he would somehow find a way to make you laugh. He had a way of putting you at ease in the most difficult of situations. No matter how bad he himself was feeling, he somehow rallied and made you feel better. He had a habit of making things about the other person, not himself. He cared about everyone else. That was the beauty of Jack. You were the most important person in the room if he was talking with you. He made you feel special and important, and yet, to a lot of people he was the special one. He never saw it that way. Not that he didn't think his life had value; he certainly did or he would have never put himself through the things he did to try to beat this cancer. He felt people, all people, were important. He made you feel that you mattered. He mattered to a lot of people, and this particular loss has been a tremendous one to our families and friends. Our losses will continue to be tremendous losses until we can learn how to deal with them in a constructive and positive way, in a way that will not be so heavy on our hearts. It will come, in our own time, and in our own ways. There is no right or wrong way to grieve. Grief is as unique as the person experiencing it. We deal with it the best we can, when we can. That is all that we can do at any given moment, and it is enough.

Jack and I were blessed with time. Some of it was difficult. I will not say it was easy; it was not. We did, however, have time. Often Jack would sit on the recliner couch and read the paper and I a book. Sometimes we talked, and sometimes we didn't. No big conversations on how to solve the problems ahead, just some quiet time together. Just being and not doing was all we needed some days. No expectations. Just being together gave us some renewed inner strength. Words, and talking about cancer, at times were not necessary. We tried to live as normal a life as we could given the situation we found ourselves in. Work, home, friends, doctor visits, chemotherapy, surgery, and all that comes with that, and somehow life got done. When we found ourselves exhausted from all of that, we found comfort in the fact that he was still here, and we still had time.

Every year on our wedding anniversary, I prayed for one more year with Jack. My prayers were answered for a long time. Even though there were times when I thought it would all be over sooner rather than later, it was not. Jack was diagnosed when we had been married twelve years. When all the odds were against us, prayers were not. Each year for the next fourteen, I found myself saying that same prayer. I just wanted one more year with the man I felt I could not live without. And it was granted.

After the wedding reception for his oldest daughter,

Shari, Jack and I were sitting on the couch, and he said, "I'd marry you all over again." Tears flooded my eyes, and I said, "Oh my god! Really?" We were married twenty-four years then. "I'm going to hold you to it!" I laughed. We renewed our wedding vows on our twenty-fifth anniversary the following spring. Reverend Tom Madden, who married us the first time, did so again for the second. It was special, very special. Our friends were there, some of whom were there the first time. It was great! We renewed our Vows, our commitment to each other, and to our faith. Time *was* on our side that day and we were blessed beyond measure. We were just two weeks shy of our twenty-sixth anniversary when Jack died. I could never complain when given so much. That's not to say I didn't cry my heart out for months after his death, I did. I missed him terribly, but however much crying was an option; complaining was not. I'm sure I did some complaining somewhere along the line about situations that came up after his death, I know me. I didn't however complain about the amount of time I had left to share with him. I had plenty of time, more than most. Take advantage of the time you have left, however much it is. Trust me, it makes a difference.

The Village Project
Jack's Favorite Project

*T*he Village Project in Bay Village, Ohio was a beautiful and very meaningful experience in both my late husband's life, and mine as well. Jack was one of Barb Harrell's, and the Village Project's, biggest fans. Barb is the VP Executive Director of the Village Project.

The Village Project was established on September 10, 2010 in Bay Village, Ohio,and was modeled after the Ceres Community Project of Sebastopol, CA. Barb had received a copy of their cookbook, *Nourishing Connections,* and learned of their innovative concept of gathering together a community which would minister to their neighbors who were in health crisis by providing them with nourishing meals.

Their Mission is to come together as a community, of all ages, and provide nourishing meals and extended care and service to their neighbors experiencing cancer.

Their Vision is to provide a vehicle to approach the devastating disease of cancer in a positive, hopeful manner by utilizing gifts and talents in a corporate and multi-generational setting to provide healthful meals, extended support, and an opportunity for all to experience the joy of serving.

Their Ideals are simply stated, yet full of purpose. They are:

Christian Witnesses - They look to Jesus as their example and then look for creative ways to offer themselves to others. They strive to grow more caring, compassionate and respectful.

Food is core; yet not a means to an end - They realize food is a basic human need and a way to initially reach out to people. However, care is extended beyond those meals.

Connect Community - They know that to be able to truly connect with others you must learn to know one another. They take the time to build relationships, care for one another and share themselves and their resources, thereby bettering their community.

Multi-Generational - The unique gifts and qualities of multiple generations are fully utilized and appreciated when combined together. When this happens, the skills and passions result in a release of contagious energy!

Full of Hope - They are confident that in the midst of our personal challenges, and there are often many, that a smile or a giggle, even a simple conversation during an act of service can, and has, for both Jack and me, brought some of the healing we needed.

Their clients come from referrals from family, friends and neighbors and sometimes from the potential client themselves. The Clients were initially from the local community, but as volunteers grew, the program grew tremendously. They are now able to serve more people both locally and in surrounding areas. Clients *and their families* are served three full meals a week for twelve weeks at no charge. After twelve weeks a monetary donation is suggested to continue receiving meals.

I can tell you from personal experience that these meals are prepared from the best available food sources. They are cooked in a special kitchen that is State Inspected. The high school students also learn to cook, and there is no fooling around! Some of these students know first-hand, from their own experience, how important this is. The meals are cooked and delivered fresh, from appetizer to dessert every one!

The added touches that came with our meals were priceless. The local Brownie Troop hand painted little glass jars and fresh flowers were placed in them and delivered with our meal. Also included with every meal was a card signed by everyone who had a part in cooking or preparing part of the meal that week. Some of these cards were handmade and beautifully decorated. All were greatly appreciated! I still have some of them that I kept when I moved. I kept them because it reminds me still, although it was a difficult time in our lives, that we were so generously loved and taken care of in such a special way by so many people. Some of whom we never met.

Jack would always ask, "Who cooked my meal this week?" and we would laugh and I would read off all the names! He knew some of them, I knew a few. It meant more to us than you could know. We knew some of the high school kids because he worked at Bay Presbyterian Church, and we attended there as well. The church was where the Village Project was originally located for the first couple of years.

I cannot say enough about the Village Project and the people who volunteer their time, talents, money and efforts to keep it going. His children are also very involved with the Village Project and I am sure he is one very proud Dad.

A percentage of the proceeds from each book sold will be donated to the Village Project in Jack's memory. This above all was his favorite cause. I will do all that I can to further this cause.

If you are able, and can find a way, please think about starting a project like this in your community. It not only will do so much good for you, but for countless others. I can tell you from personal experience, you have no idea how grateful people will be.

You can contact bharrell@ourvillageproject.com for more information. I am sure she will guide you in the right direction.

With gratitude and grace -
Kerry

Plan A

*P*eople come into our lives for a reason, a season, or a lifetime, if we're lucky. We all come with an expiration date when we are born; it's just not stamped on the bottom of our tiny feet when we get here. As we travel through our lives we lose people we love, and people who may have been mere acquaintances. We may start to question our own immortality. I certainly did. We don't know what life will bring us, nor do we know where it will take us. Life will bring us life, and it will take us to places that challenge not only our faith, but ourselves. Is life fair? We undoubtedly will question whether or not it is. Fair has nothing to do with it; life is life. It has a beginning and an end. I don't know why some people die young on their journey in life, or some old, I just know we all eventually do. I know one thing for sure, and that is that life itself is sacred.

The three words I fear most for myself and others are: You have cancer. There is nothing that strikes fear in the heart of most people than these three simple, yet complicated, words.

We were living in what I called 'Plan A', the now and present moments of our lives. Jack appeared to be the picture of health. He was active, healthy, sports oriented and had more energy than the Energizer Bunny! We were living in Florida, had great jobs, and all was well in our little world. It was in late August of 1998 on a sunny day in southwest Florida where the sun seems to make everything shine when the clouds started swiftly rolling in.

The call came that changed our lives, and everything we thought about them, sooner than anyone would have wanted or expected. The doctor's office called to say they wanted us to come in and discuss his chest x-ray. Jack always had a chest x-ray every August the week of his birthday along with a complete physical. That was not unusual for him. It's funny how some men will not go near a doctor's office and here he is making his own appointments to make sure he stays healthy. It was a good thing he did. Even though his cancer was already at Stage III-B at the time, it was caught early enough to be removed.

We were both very uneasy sitting in the waiting room with a silence still as night. Being a Registered Nurse and working on a surgical floor as well as having Oncology experience at the hospital, my gut instinct told me this was not good. I was not wrong. When his doctor gently said, "You have lung cancer" it was as if my head instantly entered a vacuum. I heard what he said; I just could not process it. I looked at Jack, sitting on the edge of the cold silver examination table. His dark navy work uniform shirt was still half buttoned after his doctor listened to his lungs. The time of 3:15 on the clock stood as still as the air. I could hear my own breath slowly going in and out. I was waiting for a reaction from Jack. He was not prepared for this. It was the farthest thing from his mind. As he sat there, almost motionless, his face drained of all emotion. I glanced at the doctor who didn't move. He waited for Jack to respond. Jack was not able to say a word. It wasn't fear that gripped him at this moment; it was sadness. A sadness that I had never seen before slowly crept across his face as the tears welled in his beautiful blue eyes. Life all of a sudden didn't seem fair. It didn't seem right. It *wasn't* right and probably never would be from that moment on. Neither of us could wrap our brains around what was being said. Jack couldn't say a word. His doctor sensed he needed to give us some time. He left the room and said he would give us a few minutes alone and then be back to talk about options. Options, a funny word when you're trying to decide what may, or may not, save your life at the moment.

"This can't be happening," Jack said with disbelief "I feel fine! I have no symptoms! This can't be happening."

"It's going to be okay Jack. It will be. They caught it early; it's going to be okay sweetheart, really. We have options." I said as I looked into those beautiful blue eyes and smiled as best I could.

Within the week the decision was made and surgery was done to remove one half of Jack's left lung. His attitude was so positive that I felt guilty not feeling the same. I acted as if all would be well when I wasn't sure any of it would be. The days in ICU with monitors, pain medications and IV drips seemed both to have flown by and at the same time drag, seeming never ending.

Working at the hospital gave me extra opportunity to sneak a few minutes here and there on my breaks and lunch hour to see him. When I went to his room it didn't matter if he was awake or asleep, I needed to physically see him. I needed to know he was breathing. I just wanted to assure myself that he was still alive and here. Alive and well was no longer the option, but alive *and here* seemed to be a blessing.

Recovery was rough. Jack had never been in a hospital

his entire life, which at this point was sixty years. Amazing what we take for granted. His thoracic surgeon told him he could go home when he was able to walk down the hallway and back to his room. He wanted out of that hospital quicker than he got into it! He walked slow but sure every day. On day five he was released home. Normally patients go home from lung surgery on day seven or eight, sometimes day ten. Not Jack, he was determined to get his life back on track. He did what he always did; he rose to the occasion and home he went.

Chest x-rays, CAT scans, and MRI's followed every three months for two years. I always secretly waited for the other shoe to drop. One had already fallen. I was only too sure that the shoelace on the other one had at least, if nothing else, been untied. On the outside I was supportive, and insistent we could, and would beat this thing. Inside, not so much.

Fear flowed through my body like morning fog on a lake in the middle of nowhere. The committee in my head had many meetings, some of which I chose to leave early. I tried to leave it in God's hands, trusting that He was somehow in the details. He had to be. Both of us needed to believe that, and we did. And He was.

A few more years passed, and although rarely spoken of, it was secretly nagging in the back of my mind. It was always there: "what if?" Fear followed me like an unseen yet very present entity. It crept in and out of my mind almost daily. No matter how busy I stayed the moment I stopped it was there. It seemed at times there was no escaping this reality. I fell asleep with it, and I woke up with it. So did Jack. We tried to block it out. We kept it positive. In reality we had no control over it. As if we really have any control over these kinds of things in the first place. We don't, or at least we didn't. What we did have control over was how we were going to try to get through it.

Jack didn't like being home recovering. He wanted to be at work, or at least with some of his friends. He wanted to play tennis again. He wanted to go to the tennis club and just sit and watch his friends play. After a few weeks he did just that. He said to me, "Get these get well cards out of here; it looks like a navy sickbay." He appreciated the fact that people were thinking about him, but it also was a reminder of what he had just gone through, cancer surgery. That he didn't want to be reminded of.

He paced himself like he was told to by his doctors and when allowed he was back at work. It gave us a sense of normalcy when he was working. He began, slowly returning to the tennis court with his friends. He was not about to give up what he loved!

Okay, now remember I told you Jack had a great sense of humor. When he was finally allowed to resume all "normal" activities he decided he wanted to make love. Okay, fast forward. He said to me,

"Oh my god you took my breath away!"

"Wow! You haven't said *that* in a while!"

"No, I mean literally! I can't breathe….."

So much for the romance. We laughed so hard. It was such a poignant moment. I love to tell that story because it was a great funny moment when we needed it.

The cancer returned just under the magical five year mark. I really don't know why we think if we make it past the five year mark we're safe. I thought that. I hoped that. I wanted it to be true for us, but it wasn't. It was back and now metastatic because the primary site had already been removed. It was a good thing we had made the decision to move back home to Cleveland two years earlier to be closer to family. Here we had access to the best medical facilities in the world. I thought to myself, Kings come here from Saudi Arabia to get treated. This is good. It had to be good. We needed it to be good.

There is nothing routine about surgery, any surgery, even at Cleveland Clinic. As large as Cleveland Clinic is, regardless of the number of surgeries they do daily, they were organized, extremely efficient, and they made it personal. If you have to go through something like this, I can tell you this is the place you would want to be. I felt like *I* mattered as much as Jack. Okay, maybe not *quite* as much as Jack, but they made sure I had everything I needed while he was in there and being taken care of. To me that's close enough!

Waiting, watching mindless television in the lobby with strangers, eating food you really don't taste and drinking coffee you really don't need becomes the norm. Having polite conversation with your husband's grown children, none in the medical field, can be taxing and challenging. It was hard not to project too much and give them more information than they were able to process. When you don't see it every day likes nurses do, and most families and friends don't, it can be frightening. It's also frightening when you do see it every day and now you are the family member and not part of the medical staff. I worked very hard on trying to be the wife and not the nurse when it came to Jack. It was hard, very hard. It was especially hard when I was a Hospice & Palliative Care Nurse for eight of those years during our fourteen year battle with this cancer.

ICU again. Chest tubes, IV drips, monitors, bells and noise became routine once more. This time it was more days. It was clear that this surgery took more out of Jack than the last.

The words "We will be treating this cancer very radically" ran through my mind over and over. What does very radically mean anyway? It's all relative. For me it meant watching the love of my life lose his hair, lose parts of his body that helped him take in the very air necessary to keep him alive, but never losing his faith. It meant waiting from March 1st of the current year to August 12th of the *following* year to learn if the surgery and chemotherapy were even successful. It was a long-acting chemotherapy. That was an understatement. Having to wait seventeen months for another scan seemed absurd to me. To his doctors it wasn't. Long-acting meant just that. We were told there was no point in scanning too early when the chemotherapy was still at work. The results would not yet be clear. So we waited, hoped, and prayed.

One night as we just laid in bed, quietly my thoughts wandered then I said to Jack, "I can't imagine my life without you…" his response was, "Then don't." What a simple concept which is anything but. Live in the moment, one moment at a time. There is an order to life in the universe. It may not be the order we chose but it is in order. We learned there is nothing more sacred than life itself. Everyone's life is sacred and it matters. Money, cars, careers and things have no value compared to the value of a life of someone you cannot imagine living your life without.

This has been my greatest lesson in this life. Learning how to love someone through a deadly illness and try not losing my faith or myself in the process. I will say that I had my faith sorely tested at times over those years and since Jack's death as well. This was not an easy journey. How could it be? Jack always had a simple faith; I on the other hand did not. It was complicated for me, very complicated. I struggled often with it. I also lost bits and pieces of me without even realizing it. That too, was okay. I also grew in areas I never knew existed. And yet, I would do it all over again to have just one, one more hour with Jack. To be able to trust that God *is* in the details, and that whatever power there is, it's on our side, even now, is a gift.

I had the honor of being married to the most marvelous man on the earth for twenty six years and see him through the most difficult challenges of his life. Being there when it counted and when it did not was a gift. It wasn't all negative, not at all! We had periods of time in remission when we had a lot of fun! Jack went back to playing tennis, working full time, and working out at the gym. He said one time, "Well, I don't play as well as Pete Sampras, but I'm back to playing tennis!" to which I answered, "You never *did* play like Pete Sampras!" to which he smiled and said: "Who *asked* you?!?" He just had the best sense of humor.

To be able to share this journey with you, and possibly help you with some suggestions on the way, is my way of giving back what so many people have given me. If you find even one thing in this book that may help you hang onto it. We all have our own way of doing things. This was just how we did it. Sometimes things worked, sometimes they didn't – but if it worked more often than not, it's in this book.

I shared these words with Jack before he died -

"I truly believe that if my only purpose for being on this earth was to see you through this difficult time in your life, then it will have been enough."

It was enough. I never really planned on being a nurse. The opportunity presented itself and I took it. I have been in healthcare for over twenty years, and I have never regretted changing careers. The career change happened long before I knew what I would go through with Jack. As a nurse I have seen many people transition from this life to the next, and although at times difficult, they were times that made me feel like what I was doing mattered. Every experience mattered; not only to me, but to the people I was with. It mattered that I cared.

Time and how we spend it is a curious thing. Abe Lincoln said, "If I had eight hours to cut down a tree, I'd spend six hours sharpening my ax." If I had eight hours to do something, chances were that, I too, would procrastinate. Not so much anymore. If your loved one is still here you are living in what I call Plan A. Plan A is the present moment. We can do nothing about the past or the future in the present moment. All we can do is what we are doing this very minute. We are living our lives one day at a time, often one hour at a time, and for some one moment at a time.

Time is a gift. If you have been given this gift I would say use it wisely. I'm not saying we have to be busy every second of every day. What I am saying is that should we use the gift of time wisely we may have less regrets in the end.

How many times have we heard someone say, "I wish I had spent more time at the office" on their deathbed? No, we don't hear that. What I have heard patients, their families and friends speak about were their regrets about not spending more time with their family or friends. I heard patients speak about the lost years of relationships that would have been more meaningful had they not held a grudge for so long. Had we not kept that anger brewing inside, wasted time with imaginary conversations in our head, repeating over and over who said what; we could have made a difference. Does it really matter? When in reality, when all is said and done, none of the petty stuff matters. People and friends matter. Family matters if you are lucky enough to have one, and I was very lucky to have mine.

Time is a gift not to be taken for granted. Taking time for family and friends is important. I am just as guilty as the next person. I have had patients tell me that they wished they had time for one more vacation, and some were lucky enough to do it. Most regretted they were not. Health declined and they couldn't do it or financially they were now beset by unexpected medical bills and it was out of the question. With Jack I have experienced both. The pressure of our financial situation escalated as his health declined. Yes, we took small weekend away day trips and one great trip to Hawaii during those years when we could. When later Jack's health deteriorated and we could no longer, we didn't. I will tell you from my personal experience that our Hawaii trip was a gift! It was after the first bout of cancer. The weekend away trips that we took to Lake James in Angola, Indiana were special, yet difficult. Difficult first, because I knew we were now living on borrowed time, and second because this was our favorite getaway place and I knew Jack loved this place since he was a child. We both loved this place, but I knew he was thinking it might be the last time he was there. He was not wrong. I knew in my heart it would be the last vacation we took for a 4th of July week there, and as difficult as it was, it was special and beautiful. We had those memories. We did what we could with the time we were given.

Before I was married to Jack I used to work my vacations. I was a single Mom with three small children. I didn't have money to go anywhere so I worked many vacation days just for the extra money. I can tell you now that I doubt my children would have minded simply going to the park with a picnic lunch and playing in the water on those days. For some reason I thought I had to *take* them somewhere or do something that cost a lot of money. I was wrong. My children are grown now, and I doubt they would have minded if we would have just stayed home. Okay, maybe not if they were teenagers, but when they were younger, I doubt they would have minded.

My son-in-law Doug, who I think is the greatest Dad on the planet, told me how he loved going to his Grandmas. He said there's a memory he has that stays with him and it's special. He would be watching TV with a little TV tray in front of him just eating crackers. But to him as a child it was very special. He just loved being with her, it didn't have to be anywhere special. Just being with her was enough. I spend time with my grandchildren, and it's special. We don't have to go anywhere for it to be special, it just is. Just a suggestion for those of you who still have little ones, or little grandchildren: a picnic basket with peanut butter and jelly sandwiches will do!

What we needed, and our children as well, were time with each other. Children of parents, and grandparents, who are ill struggle as well. They may act out or not. They may talk or not. Often it is difficult for children to put into words what they want to say. It's difficult for adults. Then, on the other hand, very young children just put it out there in their own special ways.

When Jack had been diagnosed the third time, my daughter Candy and her husband Doug brought their children from Seattle to Cleveland to see Grandpa Jack while he was still up and around. It was an amazing thing to witness when Piper, age three and a half came in just after they got there and said:

"Grandpa Jack, we came to visit you because, well, one, you have cancer and two, you're gonna die." I just held my breath for a minute.

"Yep Piper, I have cancer and yes, I'm going to die" he said with a gentle smile.

"Well, can I say a prayer for you?" She looked right at him. Her innocence melted my heart. Tears filled my eyes. What a gift!

"Of course you can Piper!" He sat down on the couch

and folded his hands. I stood in the kitchen next to Candy. Piper said her prayer, it was so precious, and we all said, "Amen!"

The next day Jack told me that Anderson, who was five, came over to him while he was drinking his morning coffee on the couch and asked him ever so sweetly:

"Grandpa Jack, is your cancer gone now?"

"No, it's still there."

"Okay, we'll pray again." It was matter-of-fact to Anderson. He thought since Piper's prayer wasn't answered overnight that he would just say another one.

I have to say that Candy and Doug talked to our grandchildren in a way where they could have some sort of understanding about what was going on. They obviously didn't know the gravity of the situation, but they did know that Grandpa Jack was sick. On their own level they knew it was serious enough for them to say prayers about. They weren't unhappy while they were there, just the opposite! We had fun! We laughed, played games, watched kid's movies and had dinner together. For a month we did that and it was great. When they left they didn't really know that it would be the last time that they would see Grandpa Jack. They were little children, and in their minds they did what *they* could - they said prayers for him. It was beautiful.

Piper was with me recently in my condo and there was a picture of Jack on my coffee table. It had been more than two years since his death. "I miss that guy you know" she said holding the picture. "Me too. I miss Grandpa Jack a lot." She set down the picture and went on to play with her doll. It was simple yet sweet. She remembers him, and she too misses him in her own little way. I don't shy away from the conversation when my grandchildren start talking about him. I let them talk, and I answer her questions.

Then, just like most little ones, their focus changes to something else.

A diagnosis by its very nature creates a new normal. When I look back at how it all happened I can say that I see the hand of God had been everywhere. I will also say that at the time of the first diagnosis, I felt it was *a very heavy* hand. I have had to come to terms with the fact that everything in life is not an Act of God.

It was life. Life on life's terms. There was nothing I could do about most of it, but some of it I had some small measure of control over. That small measure was my reaction to what was going on around me and my attitude. I had to keep my actions and reactions along with my attitude in check. I couldn't control the cancer, chemo or its side effects, the multiple surgeries and certainly not death. I had no control over the denial of some of my husband's family members and friends who, I finally realized were unable to grasp the fullness of what was going on at certain times. I was expecting too much of them. They weren't nurses that had medical backgrounds in oncology or hospice. They didn't have the experiences of death and dying I did. They didn't understand it all. How could they? It was all new to them. With every new remission came renewed hope that it was gone forever. I knew it was not. My nursing experience told me otherwise. I had to lower my expectations of them and myself. It was difficult, very difficult. I wanted things back to normal. Normal as I knew it was gone; a new normal had arrived.

You don't have to do everything at once. Some days you don't have to do anything at all if you don't want to. My suggestion would be that you don't let too many of those days build up together. If you do you may end up in a slump that will be very difficult to get out of. How do I know this? Well, because I did just that. Experience is the best teacher as we already know. I had days where I felt that I had to do everything, but I really didn't. I put those expectations on myself. No one expected me to be all things to all people, I put that on myself. It wasn't that I didn't have family and friends asking what they could do for me, I did. I always reassured people things were under control whether they were or not.

My suggestion would be this: If someone asks you if you need something and you do, say yes. I said 'no thanks, I'm good' so many times that I convinced myself that I really was ok and didn't need anything or anyone's help when I certainly did. I was not ok on so many levels some days. What I was good at was compartmentalizing my life. I was very good at that! When I was at home, I was there. When I was at work, I was there. When I was having coffee with a friend I was there. To some degree that's good, in other ways it's not.

At some point things will start to overlap. At least for me they did. It got to the point that I could no longer compartmentalize my life in little perfect boxes no matter how much I wanted to. I needed help, but I didn't want to ask for it. I was burning the candle at both ends expecting not to be caught by the fire in the middle. It didn't work. What was happening, that I could not see at first, was that I worried so long and so hard about the outcomes of so many situations that I mentally exhausted myself. I would tell myself that everything was fine. Everything was *not* fine! *I* was not fine. I had to find a way to take care of myself. I think I unconsciously did not take care of myself. I doubt it was a conscious thing. I don't think that I woke up one day and said, "Well, today I am NOT doing a thing to take care of myself at all!" That would have been ridiculous! I took showers, washed my hair, had my nails done. Hair and nails were always the big ones. I was doing all those little outside things that made me think I was ok to some degree. The outside was much easier to take care of than the inside. I could make myself smile and tell you everything is fine. I've done it a million times. I can also tell you that probably half of those million times I was, in fact, not fine at all.

It was difficult for both Jack and I to ask for help. We both saw ourselves as very competent and independent people. I am a fiercely independent woman, or so I would have you believe. Really, I am not. I like doing things if I can and hate to ask for help. That alone doesn't make one independent. It doesn't make one proud or arrogant either. It just made it harder on me. What I found was when confronted with being in a situation that is not only emotionally draining on both me and the person I loved I wanted to be the one to make it alright. It was never going to be alright, but I wanted to make it alright, and I spent a lot of time and energy trying to make it so. Physically and emotionally I crashed.

When Jack was in Cleveland Clinic for open heart surgery I was so overwhelmed. A woman I worked with, Collette Stanley, came to my office and said,

"What do you need?"

"Chocolate chip cookies. I need chocolate chip cookies and a cup of coffee. That's all I need right now."

The next day when I came in there were homemade chocolate chip cookies on my desk! I will never forget that moment because I looked at them, I took a deep breath, and for once in a long time I smiled. Those cookies were the best! They came from someone who cared enough to ask, and she baked them because I was honest enough to say I needed something. Something simple, yes. It was when I began to realize that people ask you because they want to not because they have to that I started accepting help from other people. The fact that I certainly wasn't going to be baking chocolate chip cookies anytime soon, if at all, didn't matter. Those chocolate chip cookies are one of the fond memories of my heart. I smile when I think about it. I have not seen Collette for a number of years, but that doesn't matter because she and her cookies will always be something I remember because it was one of the first times I said 'yes' to someone who asked me what *I* needed.

If the shoe was on the other foot and you needed something I would have done it for you. I am often good at helping someone out much more so than accepting help. It is so much easier for me to give than receive. I don't know why that is, but it is.

I had a very dear friend when I lived in Florida and her name was Jean. She was an older woman, many years older than me. We had lunch weekly, we talked a lot, and she was just a joy to be around! I remember one day we went to lunch and she insisted on picking up the check. I argued against it, and then she said with a big smile, "Two words are sufficient." I looked at her for a minute, and then I realized what she was getting at. I simply said, "Thank You." I have never forgotten that moment over twenty years ago, and I smile when I think about it. When people pay for my lunch and I want to say no, or I pick up the check and someone else wants to say no, I simply say, "Two words are sufficient" and smile.

I have found that most of us do things because we want to not because we have to. Let us continue to do things for each other, friends and strangers alike. Not because we have to, but because we want to.

I have taken care of hundreds of patients over the years I have been a nurse, and it was an honor to do so. I can honestly say that, although I may not have realized it at the moment, each one has impacted my life in one way or another. Some have made me laugh, some made me cry, some made me throw my hands up in the air after I left the room wondering what in the world was going on with them. Hindsight is always 20/20.

I learned how to know what was going on with patients when I learned how to listen to them. Not just listen to what they were saying, but what they were not. People can tell you a lot of things verbally, and they can tell you more with their body language. As nurses we learned how to tell if a patient is in pain by using verbal and nonverbal pain scales. I believe it is the same way with emotions. People can tell you, and sometimes they will, if they are in a lot of emotional pain. Sometimes you can not only see the pain, but you can *feel* it if you are in tune with them. It took practice.

Not only are patients feeling physical and emotional pain, their families and friends are as well. I would venture to say that we all know someone, or possibly we ourselves, are or have been, in a situation that is both physically and emotionally draining. I know I have. In nursing we are taught to keep boundaries in these areas. Boundaries are hard to keep when you get attached to people and families you work with whether in a hospital or a hospice setting, but they are there for a reason. The staff has to keep their focus on the job at hand to keep the patient and family as healthy and as comfortable as possible and use the best practices they can.

What happens then, when you *are* a nurse and your husband is diagnosed with Stage III-B Lung Cancer? That was the question I had to ask myself when it happened to me. I was working in a hospital setting on a surgical floor and also had some oncology experience. I knew that Stage III-B Lung Cancer was serious. The stages only go to IV. I knew I somehow had to figure out how to leave what I knew as a nurse out of it, which basically seemed impossible. I had to focus on how to be the wife and not the nurse in this scenario. I'm glad to have figured it out. So if you are in Plan A remember you are not alone. There will be many things to deal with. You will deal with them, hopefully, with gratitude and grace.

On Going Forward - As Franklin D. Roosevelt once said, "There are many ways of going forward but only one way of standing still." We need not stand still. Going forward takes courage. Sometimes it takes a lot of courage. There will be days when you feel you can't take one more step forward. That's okay, then don't. Stop! Take a breath and regroup. Everyone needs to regroup at times. No one can keep going day after day without stopping and taking a bit of time out.

The first time Jack was diagnosed we felt rather lucky. Jack had surgery within the week and half of his left lung was removed. We were told basically to 'enjoy our life' as it were. It was overwhelming to me the first time and to Jack as well. We did just that, we enjoyed our lives. He went back to work and it was business as usual. Well, as much as it can be at that point. It's never business as usual. Once cancer is in your house and mind it never leaves. You think it's gone, and for Jack - well, he was in remission for a few good years. It was always in the back of his mind. It never left my mind from the day he was diagnosed.

The second time the cancer returned it was just under the magical five year mark. Jack was stunned. I was not. I was angry. Again more surgery and now chemo, long acting at that, more rehab, and back to work, etc. Downsizing our life again. We simplified everything we could to keep things simple. It was a daily battle for a longer period of time now. Recovery wasn't so quick now.

Jack did eventually go back to work but it was harder on him this time. It was getting emotionally harder now for both of us.

When Jack and I decided, the third time he was diagnosed that we would keep going forward, I have to say it was tough. The third time the cancer returned we were pretty much out of options. When there are no more options it all comes down to attitude. How you're going to live out your days, not necessarily months or years, matters. It matters a lot.

We knew we were on thin ice by now. Having been diagnosed fourteen years earlier we No one lives fourteen years with lung cancer - not normally, anyway I sat there stunned as the doctor at Cleveland Clinic said, 'We're going to make you comfortable. We can't fix it this time.' I wanted to cry. I did everything I could not to. Tears welled in my eyes, my stomach was in knots, and I felt like I was in another time and place. I clearly heard what was being said, I just could not process it. I felt sick. I was, for the first time in all of this, speechless. I, the Hospice Nurse had been the one who had said those very words over and over to my patients for years, and now I am on the other side of it hearing them. *Really* hearing them for the very first time. It was as if someone was telling me something that could not possibly be true. How could it be? I didn't want it to be; therefore it couldn't be. Or so it seemed.

Jack wanted to try another experimental treatment. The doctor said, 'Sure, whatever you want'. I could have hugged that doctor at that very moment! He knew it wouldn't work, but he knew Jack needed to try it anyway. He did two more rounds of chemo and his body could take no more.

"Kerry, I can't do this anymore. I'm sorry..." his voice cracked and his eyes filled with tears.

"You don't have to do this Jack, I love you! This chemo is destroying you. It's okay." We both knew what that meant.

"What are we going to do now? How are we going to get through this?"

"We are going to get through this with gratitude and grace Jack. We have been so blessed these past fourteen years! No one I know has been given this much time and we've done everything we've wanted to and pretty much said everything we wanted to say. We can't ask for anything more." I too felt like I was dying.

"I agree..." he smiled and kissed me on the cheek, "gratitude and grace it is!"

That was, by far, the most difficult conversation we had since day one. We were talking about the end now. We were now out of options, at least traditional treatment options. We had options about how we were going to do it. It was Comfort Care time and it sickened me inside. I now knew firsthand what my patients and their families had felt. It was the hardest day of my life.

We got through it. I say *we* got through it with gratitude and grace. Jack got through it with a *lot* of gratitude and grace. And well, if the truth be told, and this is the truth, I'm still working on it. He would have smiled at that. I say 'we' because no one goes through this process alone. Did we know at the start we would have fourteen years? Absolutely not. Not in a million years would we have ever dreamed that. You take what you can get, and we were blessed with a lot of time. Time well spent while we were together. We still had our jobs and family responsibilities, but we also spent more time together.

Jack would always say to me, "Gratitude is an Attitude". He was so right. He lived it. He was a man who walked how he talked. He enjoyed his life. It wasn't all great. There were times it was downright awful. It was excruciating to watch him recover at times let alone to be him living it. There are times that people living with cancer are more pained living with it than we are of watching it, and yet they do not complain. He never complained. Never. His attitude about life kept him, and me, going in difficult times. His outlook was positive. He fought to live, and he fought hard when he was able. That's not to say he didn't have his moments. Of course he did. He was human. I suspect I had more 'moments' than he did, or at least I was a bit more vocal about them anyway. Even so, we always moved forward. We had to. To stand still would have been devastating for either of us. When one of us was down we picked each other up. We just tried not to be down at the same time.

Moving forward one step at a time is all we can ask of ourselves. Sometimes, that too, may be too much to ask on any given day. It's okay. At those times we learn to rest in what is. We regroup and when we are ready we again step on the path of this journey. No one I've met has kept going twenty four hours a day. It's not possible. We need to be refreshed, restored, and rejuvenated for the tasks at hand. We need to take time for self-care.

There are no wrong choices when it comes to dealing with grief. We make the best choice we can at the moment, and it is, and will be, good enough.

I tend to think that I should have been over some things, as it were, regarding some of the people who have been gone from my life for some time now. What I have found is that I will never be *over* any of it; I have gotten *through* a great deal of it, and I will get through the rest of it as it comes. I did find however, that I was not able to get through it alone. I don't think it's possible to do it alone. At least for me it has not been. I have had and continue to have a host of friends and a support system that is unmatched to anything I have ever had in my lifetime. If I choose to do it alone and isolate, I suppose I could do that, but then I risk getting stuck and not able to get through anything. And to be honest, yes there are times I have done just that. I have chosen to be alone in my grief because I felt either I had talked too much about it already or I thought in my own head that people may had been tired of hearing me. I never asked so I didn't really know. People are gracious, but they aren't mind readers. They reached out to me in many ways, and many a time I said I was fine when I simply was not. I was stuck in my head. I cried a lot, and I sat alone with my thoughts a lot and I felt stuck. Stuck is not where I wanted to be. It's not where I want you to be either. It's not where we should be. Left to my own devices, I would be in a desolate and lonely place. No, stuck and isolated is not good for any of us.

Life is not meant to be endured although at times it may certainly feel that way. Life is meant to be shared. I have often heard that a problem shared is a problem cut in half. Well, maybe. I don't know that my problems were cut in half when shared, but I can say that talking with someone even just a little, had taken a bit of the emotional pressure off. My problems and concerns were still there, I just ended up with a different perspective when I was able to share them with someone I trusted.

Grief, although shared, is also at times a solo journey. There are places you will go alone and you may be afraid or scared. These are the places deep in your heart that no one knows are there but you. You will be okay. They are the places where the memories of your heart are held sacred. Places, where no matter what happens to you in life, no one can touch. They are magical places. Memories shared with your loved one that no one else has shared are right there with you. Confidences you held, even after death, are held there. If a hurricane, fire, flood or tornado took away every photo album you or I ever had it would make no difference because what matters is what is stored in the memory of our hearts.

You and I will visit and revisit these places when we are ready. I have laughed and I have cried, and I will do so again. I revisit my heart over and over to remember the good things. I am grateful to have had the memories to hold in this safe place. I will someday just smile without the tears. That day *will* come for each of us. Of that I am certain. I know this because when I first started writing this book I shed a lot of tears over both the sweet and sad memories in my heart. The tears fall less often now as I move through my life in a different way. Yes, I have my days and my moments and thankfully they are less often. Thankfully they are also less intense than when I first began this journey. I trust that you also will find less intense and less grief-filled days on your journey forward as have I.

The Shadow Lands

*O*n Grief - My friend Patty said to me: "When Jack passes it will be the hardest thing you will have ever experienced in your life." She was not wrong. Grief is as unpredictable as my friend said it would be. She has already gone through this process; she knew firsthand what it was like.

The valleys of grief are what I call the Shadow Lands. The dark places we go unattended. They are as real to us as the sun, moon, and the stars. They can be scary places. Often I have found myself in one of these valleys not quite sure how I got there, and sometimes I wasn't sure how to get out. Sometimes I was not afraid, but there were times I feared what was to come. Shadows are like fears; they loom large in our minds. When the wind blows hard and death knocks on our door we are afraid to answer. When I was a child some of my family members would make fun of me calling me a "Scaredy cat". I was not scared, there were just things I didn't understand, and people didn't take the time to explain them to me. I believe that most people are less fearful if they know what to expect. Unless you have gone through the death of someone close to you before how can you know what to expect?

My journey with grief started in mid- August of 1998. It was the day Jack got his first diagnosis of cancer. Grief doesn't start the day someone dies; it starts when you hear the diagnosis. For me it started with anticipatory grief. I was anticipating what I would miss in the future. My head went from diagnosis to no husband in a hurry. I had to rein myself in and try to stay in the moment. When you start asking yourself a million questions about what's going to happen next and the great "what if" questions, you can drive yourself crazy. The questions don't really ever seem to stop. What stops is the craziness when you take only one thing at a time. All the questions don't need to be answered right away. On a need to know basis, you only need to know, and deal with, one thing at a time. Trust me on this one. When you need the answers they will be there. We may not be able to stop the questions but we can stop predicting the outcomes. We don't really know the outcomes; those are in God's hands. We didn't know that Jack would live for another fourteen years after his first diagnosis. I will say it *was* a miracle. We still had a lot of good times while he was in remission, so my worrying about the future and what would happen, and where and when didn't matter. Worrying didn't help, it did however increase my anxiety.

I have gone through some significant losses, and so have many people before me. I lost both my brothers and my Dad prior to my husband's death. They were different in the sense that I had not shared my world with them like I did Jack. I had never been as close to anyone as I was Jack. My Dad died when I was eighteen of lung cancer. They didn't have the treatments we have today. I was close to my Dad and I still miss him terribly to this day. It took me years to really grieve that death. I was young and it was sad. Very sad.

My oldest brother Billy died nine months later at the age of twenty three of an overdose of heroin. It was in the 70's and a lot of people were coming back from Vietnam messed up on drugs. He was no different. Two losses in nine months was a lot to handle. There seemed to be no closure to Billy's death. My mother was so angry that she refused to deal with it at all. Billy was in San Diego, just coming back home from his second tour in Vietnam. She was in such denial that she refused to believe he was dead. The coroner personally called her. It didn't matter. I think as a Mom it was too much for her to take. After all, Billy had done two tours in Vietnam and survived that. Now he's stateside and he dies. She wouldn't tell us where he was or what happened, other than the overdose. When I asked what we were going to do about it she said "Nothing! Let his druggie friends bury him." I suppose they did; I don't really know. Now that's anger. At least with my Dad's death there was a funeral. I was there and I knew it was real. With Billy it seemed to be so crazy. The one thing that did give me closure was when I was in a guided meditation with a group of people at church and he appeared in my meditation. It was calming. I had a sense of clarity about the situation. Even though I don't know where he's buried to this day, and my mother has since passed on, I can only trust that all is well. When my younger brother Buddy took his life at age 36 it was rough. There was a Memorial Service so there was some closure. With Buddy I understood why he took his life. I didn't like it, but I understood it. I think of them often. I pray that they are all at peace.

When I lost Jack it was clearly different. I felt I was somewhat prepared, however when it happened, I fell apart. I was sad for a long time. The first year was filled with valleys for me. I had literally moved across the country. I started a new job, rented a condo, and was on my own for the first time in my life. It was scary. I was angry, not at Jack, but at the lung cancer. I felt it had robbed us of our future. Sometimes, even when we know it's coming, we feel unprepared. Maybe, if we're lucky we *are* prepared to some degree. We do the best we can with what we have at any given moment, and it is enough.

Grief is not pain, but grief can cause pain. Grief for me is more of an emotional pain. It certainly has also caused me physical pain. The type of pain that I'm talking about is when you cry from your heart, and you feel like you can't breathe. You cry so much your ribs ache. That kind of pain. When I've cried so much and couldn't eat or sleep, I got headaches. My stomach churned. Yes, grief can cause pain both emotional and physical.

It's been said that people can die of a broken heart. As a nurse, I believe that. I didn't think that I would die of a broken heart because I felt that it was my Soul that shattered when Jack died. There are many instances of people who have been married sixty or seventy years and die within a day of each other. I have seen it in my nursing practice. It doesn't surprise me. I have had that deep in your gut pain caused by emotions. I have had the times where I cried myself to sleep night after night after Jack died, waking up exhausted. There were days when I cried all day and nights I cried all night. There is no wrong way to grieve. It takes what it takes for each of us.

There are many kinds of grief just as there are many ways to experience it. Grief can be solitary or shared. There is anticipatory grief, which is the kind of grief you feel when you are living with someone that has a long term illness. My anticipatory grief started the day Jack was diagnosed. Life literally changed in an instant. My mind went to places that were dark and deep in the first few weeks after his first diagnosis. I knew there would be things we were not going to be able to do, and things that I would be doing without him. It was hard, confusing, frustrating, and I was filled with so much emotion.

I felt a lot of emotions in my grief. I, on the one hand felt angry, and on the other anxiety. I felt like the shoes were dropping and I couldn't stop them. My mind was filled with 'what if's' and 'when'. *When* was the word that I never had an answer to. *When* put me into anxiety and tears in a heartbeat. Not only was Jack's life changing, mine was as well. I was losing the love of my life and I wanted to know *when* so I could somehow try to prepare myself. I was losing hopes and dreams, vacations, and sunsets at Lake James together. I cried a lot, not in front of Jack at first, but in the shower. No one could hear me in the shower with the fan running. I was trying to prepare myself for this loss, but unbeknown to me I had fourteen years to do it. Sometimes it felt like a lifetime, and I felt like I couldn't absorb one more thing. It gave us time for closure, but it also at times made me a nervous wreck. I always felt on edge. When I think about it I really don't know how we made it through fourteen years of it. I say we because we were both grieving the loss. Jack was grieving the loss of not only his life with me, but his children and his grandchildren, and he was dealing with losing his own life. He was facing his own mortality head on.

When Jack's granddaughter Sammy was getting ready to graduate from High School he would say, "I have to make it to Sammy's graduation." When he was in the hospital for the last time, Susan, Sammy's Mom came in and she had pictures of Sammy in her Prom dress. She asked Jack if he wanted to see them now or wait to see her in it when she was going to the Prom. He said, " Let me see it now." Jack didn't get the chance to see her in that beautiful gown in person, nor did he make it until her graduation. He passed away a week after he left the hospital.

There were days and weeks that were a blur to me. We worked pretty much throughout this entire time, until we could no longer. I think that was our saving grace. Having to focus on our jobs kept our minds off of it for at least eight to ten hours a day.

Short-lived grief is known as abbreviated grief. The grief process can seem shorter because there was a period of anticipatory grief that a person went through and is able to deal with the loss more quickly. Grief can also be delayed or chronic.

Chronic grief can lead to depression. I believe that some depression exists in the very nature of grief itself, whether it is anticipatory or delayed. I would venture to say we are at a higher risk of depression with chronic grief. You may have a period of grieving where you just can't seem to move forward. You feel stuck in your grief. It may feel like you are depressed all the time. That's different from delayed grief where maybe a person's reaction of the loss isn't right away because they are either consciously or subconsciously avoiding the reality. They are unable to allow the experience of emotional pain that goes with grief and therefore suppress it. We may just want things to be the way they were before and are unable to adjust to what is right now.

There is also grief that is considered distorted, and grief that can be masked. Grief that is masked is when a person is unable to function normally and is unable to recognize that the symptoms can present as physical symptoms or maladaptive behaviors.

It can be that symptoms and reactions to the loss are extreme and intense. Self-destructive behavior and odd behavior fall under this category as well. Intense anger and hostility turned either inward toward you or outward toward others is not unusual.

Wherever you may be in the grief process you do not have to be there alone. You can certainly choose to be alone. A lot of people are not able to let their guard down in front of others for fear of feeling vulnerable. That's okay. As I mentioned, grief can be solitary or shared. There are things I grieved openly and things I did not. As much as I tried to keep a stiff upper lip, for me it wasn't always possible. I also felt that I should have been 'done with this' by now. I told myself that after all, fourteen years of it should certainly have been enough for anyone. I was wrong.

On Depression - I suffered many, many bouts of depression during those fourteen years. If the truth be told, and this is the truth, there were days I wished *I* could be the one to leave this planet. I clearly didn't want to be here anymore. There were days when I would be driving home after work on the freeway at night and wanted to keep on driving. It didn't matter where; I just wanted to keep driving. I wanted to drive until I either ran out of gas, money, or was simply exhausted. I never did it, but I certainly wanted to. I hated what was happening in my life. I didn't feel I could keep doing what I was doing. However, I would do it all over again to have Jack back for just one day. But back then I didn't feel like I could keep on doing it much longer. But I did. That happened three years before Jack died.

There was a particular time, just a few days after Christmas one year that I fell into the worst depression I had known. It started probably long before I noticed it, but for me it culminated in one awful week. I came home from work one night and announced that I hated my life! I told Jack that I loved *him* more than anything, which I did, but I hated what was going on in my life. I also mentioned something about taking a handful of pills if I had enough of them because I didn't want to even wake up the next morning. When I got up the next morning Jack was sitting in his chair in the living room.

"What time did you get up?" I asked.

"I've been up all night, just sitting in this chair."

"Why?"

"Why? You come home from work and tell me if you had a hand full of pills you'd take them and you ask me 'Why?' I was afraid that's why. I didn't want anything to happen to you."

"Oh. I'm not angry at you, I love you. I'm just tired of my life. I'm tired of the cancer. I'm tired of worrying about the future. I'm tired of watching you go through all these treatments and it just keeps coming back."

"I called Tom Madden" he said gently. He knew that Tom, our Pastor could help. He also knew if there was anybody I trusted it was Tom.

"He's going to call you."

"Okay, I'll talk to him."

Tom called not long after and asked me what was going on. I was sure Jack had already told him but I told him, but I told him how I felt anyway. He asked me if I was taking my antidepressants. I said yes. It evidently wasn't helping. Tom asked me if he could say a prayer for me. I agreed to that. I wasn't sure if God was in all of this mess, but I felt it couldn't hurt. Since it appeared to me that my prayers were falling on deaf ears, at least Tom had a hotline to God, or so I felt. Tom said a prayer in his very calming voice and I breathed a little easier. He prayed that I would have peace. "The peace that passes all understanding" he said. I did feel at peace. He suggested I call my Psychiatrist, right now, and talk with her. I did and was in her office within two hours. It took time to get through that depression, and it wasn't easy. I have never forgotten that particular prayer, and when I'm struggling I just ask God for that peace, the peace that passes all understanding, and it makes a difference.

I had a different type of grief after Jack died. I wouldn't necessarily say it was abbreviated grief. More than two years later something might trigger me and I still can cry at the drop of a hat. No, that was not abbreviated. It was more cumulative if anything.

Grief is as individual as we are. There is no right or wrong way to grieve. We do it in our own time, in our own way. I got a lot of outside help. I needed it, and I wasn't ashamed that I did. I found that talking to Psychologists and Therapists helped. Actually, I talked with a few great ones during and after my own loss. Psychologists are great listeners, not because you pay them to be, but because they care. Rob Chwast, PhD, was the Psychologist who helped me deal with the anticipatory grief first. He actually put a name on it for me. I had said in one session, "I feel like I'm sitting on a time bomb." His answer was, "you are." He was right. I saw him for quite some time and it helped me immensely. David Ackerman, LISW-S, MSSA another therapist, whom I saw until I left Cleveland, was a godsend to me. He was there for me literally at the drop of a hat. Jack would joke that I had him on speed dial! We laughed about it, but David was my lifeline to sanity. I would talk and cry and talk and laugh, then cry some more. Neither David nor Rob ever judged me. That was the beauty of it. I felt safe to talk about my fears and I knew they weren't going to leave those offices. I could get it off my chest and the burden was lighter every time I did. I would recommend it to anyone. I truly believe that as intense as it was at times my grief was made easier by these two therapists. That's not to say it was lessened, they *softened* it. Sometimes what we need is for someone to soften for us what feels so harsh. They both did that for me, and for these two men I will be forever grateful. There is nothing wrong with getting professional help when you need it. It certainly got me through some of the toughest times of my life.

On Walking - Beware of wanting to run through the Shadow Lands. Running is not a good idea. Walk, don't run. Grief is a process whether we like it or not. It would be great if we could skip some of these things, but for some reason all of them appear necessary. I don't know why, other than we're just human. Being human and wanting to be understood, yes, even in our grief we will need to trust that others have been there before us and have survived.

We can't outrun cancer or any other illness. It always seems to have a way of catching up to us. It's exhausting to try. We can't win that race - I've tried along with many others. Yes, you can try, and you may, like I did, but you will not win. What you *can* do is walk. Put one foot in front of the other no matter the pace, but walk. You may have days when you feel you can't take one more step. I have had those days, and sometimes when grief hits me seemingly out of nowhere I still do. At that point stop. Just stop where you are and let it be. It's okay. There will be more steps to take, and more days to take them. You will take them; just not today.

On Family - Sharing our grief with someone can be a welcome relief to us, and them as well, especially before a funeral. Our friends feel a need to help. They want to do something to ease our pain. Although sometimes families aren't exactly at their best when it comes to funerals, we still need to walk through it. Planning a funeral, especially an unexpected one can be daunting. I was blessed to have my family with me and Jack's family as well. I was blessed to be able to say what I needed to say to Jack's grown children and they understood. There was no arguing over funeral plans, no distress over who was or was not talking to whom. It was actually the best that it could have been given our circumstances. There are people that know you so well that you don't have to say a word. You can just be. It was that way with my sister Kathy. My daughter Candy and my nephew Ben couldn't have made it any easier. They were great. I realize it's not always that way with families. I have seen, and in my own family experienced, some bizarre behavior. Not at Jack's funeral thank God, but that of my younger brother Buddy. Some family members were not talking to each other. My Mom was in such denial of what was going on we were walking on eggshells. No one wanted to upset her any more than she was already. Now, try to plan a funeral when you have the Mom denying everything about the situation. Not only were we walking on eggshells we had to walk through it together for her sake. It was not easy. I just wanted to run. I wanted to be so far away from that experience that I can't even tell you how I felt. All I knew was that I didn't want to be there. I wanted to be someplace, anyplace, but where I was. I wanted to run, but I could not. I needed to walk through this funeral and have some closure for myself.

We have to understand, no matter how fractured a family is, and mine was no exception, we are *all* grieving the same loss. Yes, each in our own way, but we are all still in grief. Some of us want to be alone; others want to be surrounded by people. Whether or not we share our thoughts and who we share them with is ultimately up to us.

In my nursing career I have been with families that would not call a particular family member because they were at odds over something that happened years ago. That does not mean that the person who is ill, or has died, wasn't important to them as well. We can't go through an impending death or a funeral leaving people that were important to our loved one out of the loop. No matter what the situation is, we need to rise above it and include everyone. It can be very difficult to do, but I can tell you from my own experience that when my older brother Billy died from an overdose of drugs and my Mom's response was "Let his druggie friends bury him", and when there was no funeral I was devastated. I wanted to have a funeral for him. I needed closure and it wasn't there. I had no information other than the little bit she reluctantly shared and she refused to share any more. That was difficult. It was hard to let that go. We need to realize that we aren't the only person who loved this person. No matter what our relationships with the rest of the family are we will have experienced the loss differently. Let us be sensitive to this fact.

Anger is quick in some families; forgiveness is not. Mine was no different. My relationship with my Mom was never a great one. I will tell you though, when I had the chance to change it in my own small way I did. My Mom and I were talking on the phone one day and for some reason she mentioned that she had absolutely nothing of my Dads'. They divorced when I was young. Although she married a few times after that I knew she would love him until the day she died. I had a picture of my Dad when he was younger and they were first together. I took it and had a copy of it made. I framed it and I mailed it to her with a card that said: "I know I'm not the only one who still loves him." I didn't do this because I'm a saint by any means. I did it because I knew I had something she would have wanted. My Dad died years ago at the age of

50, she was now in her 80's. She was not aware that I had these pictures. She put it on her nightstand, and there it stayed until the day she died. It was a simple gesture, but to her it was the world. No matter how the relationship looks on the outside there's always an inside story as well. It took me years to have a relationship with her at all, for reasons I won't disclose here, but when all was said and done I knew she needed that picture. If you have adult children, and/ or you have a blended family, I just ask you to please consider everyone's feelings. If the shoe were on the other foot none of us would want to be left out. It matters, and it matters a lot more than you may realize. Forgiveness is giving up the idea that the past could be anything different than it was.

Each person needs to say what they need to while people are still living. This is especially true of the person who is dying. There are a lot of times when we have a chance to make amends with family and make things right and we don't for some reason do it. This is not one of them. There are no do-overs in funerals, those are final. So again I say, consider everyone. We all need the chance to say our goodbyes. It seems that death can make or break family relationships. Just think about it. Walk alongside each other and support each other the best way you can with gratitude and grace. You will be glad you did.

On Acceptance - Acceptance of something does not mean you have to like it. I have found many times I have had to accept things I did not want to accept; feel feelings I did not want to feel. It's not easy. I can say that it gets easier with time because feelings can be both volatile and emotional. When feelings got volatile and emotional I needed to remind myself that fighting what is does not change what is. I eventually ended up at square one again. I found myself there often.

Let me share with you a moment of acceptance I had. It was a major point of acceptance in my life. I knew when I took off my wedding rings it was an acceptance of what is. What was is gone; what is, remains. It wasn't a betrayal of my love for Jack; I loved him long after he died. Nor did it mean I loved him any less. It simply meant I was well aware of the fact that I no longer felt married. I knew I wasn't married; no one needed to remind me. Of that I was well aware. I also knew in the sacred space of my heart, where I hold all things precious, that it was time. You may or may not take that step to take your rings off; it's a very personal decision. It is your decision and whichever way you decide that's okay. I thought long and hard before I did it.

I woke up on a Friday morning, not quite a year after Jack died and felt different. I wasn't quite sure I could put my finger on it, but somehow I felt different. I went to work, and I realized after a few hours what it was. I knew I was no longer married. Granted, I had been a widow for almost a year at that time, but that itself did not make me feel unmarried. For some time I had still felt married. It was odd, because that Friday morning I did not. I called my sister Kathy.

"You're going to think I'm crazy when I say this, but I don't feel married anymore." I hesitated.

"You're not crazy. It takes time to come to come to that realization. So many things happened to you all at once. You experienced a death; you moved across the country, you started a new job. It's not crazy at all."

"I feel like I want to take my wedding rings off. I did it before and ended up putting them right back on. It didn't feel right. Now it feels right."

"Then, take them off" she said gently, "put them away. If you feel you need to put them back on then do. Do what you need to do for you. Only you know what's good for you. Everybody's different."

I said a prayer and I took off my rings and I let Jack go. I did not banish him from my heart or mind, he will always be here with me. I took my rings off so that I, myself, could move on in my life as a single woman on my own.

I believe it was more symbolic than anything else. I felt it was necessary for me to let go in a physical sense with the rings. Looking at them made me somehow feel married. People would complement me on such a beautiful ring and I would smile and thank them, never mentioning that I wasn't married anymore. Saying I was a widow could possibly invite an uncomfortable moment for either of us. Now that possibility was off the table.

When people ask me if I'm married I simply say no. If I feel the situation warrants a little more of an answer then I can add to it. I am good with giving less information when I don't feel like explaining anything. We don't have to explain anything. Being a widow or widower can be very difficult. Depending where we are with our grief we just may not feel up to going into detail about it. There is nothing wrong with that. Our feelings are just that - our feelings. We can choose to keep them close some days and share them on others. There are no rules to grief.

When it comes to the loss of children it can be difficult. We are not expected to bury our children. Our children are supposed to bury us. If you are unfortunate to have lost a child you may have kept their room untouched for quite some time. You may have wanted to keep it exactly the way it was when they were here. The world around us has been moving on since we have lost our loved ones we just may not have joined them yet. If we are standing still in time, or we keep looking back, maybe, just maybe, we can reconsider where we are right now. I believe we instinctively know when we are standing still. We may be doing it out of fear, anxiety or simply just not knowing how to put one foot in front of the other. It doesn't matter why you never moved Teddy the bear off the bed, or the hairbrush off the dresser. What matters is that if you are ready to move forward, even a few little steps at a time. It will be your move and you will do it in your way. No one else can take those steps for us. Sure, people may feel uncomfortable if we have left a child's room exactly the way it was for quite some time. My late brother's wife has done that with my nephew's room after he died. For her, she needs to do this. It's ok to not pick up the baseball and glove off the floor where they left it. Does it mean you're crazy? No, it doesn't. It means you're still grieving and you will move it when you can. Grief takes time, sometimes more time than we would like or imagine. Acceptance of where we are in the process is important. *Self*-acceptance is also important. We move forward when we are ready and not a minute sooner. The earth has been here billions of years; it will be here one more day, one more week, or even one more month. Whatever time it takes for us to move that baseball and glove off the floor, well, that's what it takes. We cannot rush grief, it is a process. We can however learn to accept our grief as a journey we must go through to get on the other side of it.

On Respect - I have known families that have cleaned out entire closets the day of a funeral because they felt their parent shouldn't have to do it. My thought on it is this – there's wisdom in asking first. There's a respect that is due. A grieving widow or widower, or parent of a child needs to have the opportunity to say yes or no on it first. It's not ours to do so *we* feel more comfortable; that belongs to someone else. My sister Kathy Anne helped me clean out Jack's things *after* I asked her to. She had suffered a similar loss years before. She also knew how difficult it would be for me to do this on my own. My nephew Ben was a godsend. He drove down from upstate New York to be there with me and do whatever it was I needed, and for support. I knew I couldn't clean out Jack's bathroom. I walked in there, saw his razor on the sink, and the tears started flowing gently down my cheeks. As I stood there in the doorway I remembered the smell of the soap he used. It seemed to linger in the air. I pictured him standing there shaving at his sink just smiling at me. His powder blue towel was on the towel rack just where he left it. It felt raw. I just could not do it; not any of it. Ben took care of it all the way down to the marine life shower curtain with dolphins and fish. Jack loved dolphins. They were everywhere in our apartment. *He* was everywhere in our apartment. Kathy helped me with his closets. I stood there for a minute and told her what few items I wanted to keep and we set them aside. The rest was donated. She took them all to the donation center for me. That was something I would not have been able to do either. It was hard. It was emotional, like going down memory lane. I bit my lower lip, took a deep breath, and moved on.

I had to go through things a few days after Jack's funeral because I was moving to Seattle. That had been the plan for some time now. Even though I knew it was coming, when it got here it was a different ballgame. It was emotional, yes, much like I imagined it would be. It was difficult to let go of things that I had bought for Jack for an anniversary present or a birthday present. I had to keep telling myself that I was circulating it back into the Universe and that someone else could make good use of it. There were an awful lot of things for someone else to make good use of, that was for sure. The floor in the extra bedroom was filled with stacks of clothing that were going to one place or another. He would have laughed when I said to my sister, "Man! He has more clothes than me!" He always teased me when I went shopping saying, "Oh, what else couldn't you just live without?" And we would laugh. It makes me smile right now as I write this. I accepted that fact that it needed to be done and I knew when we were done that everything was going where it needed to go. That didn't mean everything was fine now, and that I was ok, I wasn't.

Even though we had downsized multiple times, it seemed as if the packing never stopped. I had to make decisions about what I was going to move across the country and what I was not. It was hard to let go of things. We had twenty six years of 'things' and I didn't want to let go of a lot of it. I knew I needed to let go of some of it. After all, I didn't even have an apartment yet, let alone a job! I didn't want to do this piece of it alone, and I didn't have to and neither do you. I accepted the fact that I was not okay even though I really ached to be. I was clearly not as strong as I thought I was. That was okay, I didn't need to be. None of us need to be. We aren't here by design to be strong and alone. It doesn't work that way. When I needed to be strong I said a prayer, hoped it worked and moved on. Knowing I was supported made a huge difference. I'm not sure how people do it by themselves, yet they do. Some people just want to be alone with their grief and pain. At times I felt the same way, but not all the time. Going through tough times somehow made me feel stronger in hindsight. This was just a tough time. A *very* tough time, but I knew it wouldn't last forever; nothing does. It was only going to last for about the time it took to get Jack's closet cleaned out, go through the memories as I chose to take some things and donate others, and for however long I wanted to dwell on it.

I thought about a few things I may have wanted to save for 'someday' and then I had to laugh at myself. I know me all too well. Okay, I admit to having found boxes of stuff, I had no idea what, in my storage locker that had been there still unopened from two moves ago! That's why there are thousands upon thousands of attics, basements, garages, and crawl spaces across America filled with boxes of stuff we just can't live without. Obviously we aren't living *with* it either! So for me, that 'someday' that I might need it or want it really never comes. I bet I'm not alone here either. Do what you can, and if you really aren't sure, and you have a place to store things you may just want to hold onto it for a while to go through it when you aren't as emotional. There's one thing about time, it never seems to end. You don't have to rush. When you can accept that you need to take care of things, you will.

Again, I would ask family members and friends to consider asking before you remove anything from closets or start cleaning out drawers. We know which items we want to keep and what we can let go of. It has to be our decision. It is a matter of respect. Respect for the personal belongings of the person who has passed, and respect for the ones who are still here.

Emotions Up and Down

*O*n Guilt - I have often said that guilt it a useless emotion. Guilt can destroy your peace of mind. Oh, you can keep the guilt if you want….but at what cost? I think we can unwittingly take on guilt. Some people have the ability to have you take on *their* guilt when you don't need to. It's useless; it serves no purpose. When people can get you to feel guilty then they can get what they want out of you pretty quickly. We learn it young, ask any child or teenager. People can, and will get what they want from you if you bite. Don't bite! You have enough to deal with let alone taking on something you don't need. Families are especially great at the whole guilt routine. I used to have a small button that said, "My Mother Was A Travel Agent For Guilt Trips". Really! She could send you flying on a guilt trip anywhere and everywhere. She was great at it. After all, she knew my buttons - she installed them!

Okay, so I have a little funny story about that. My Mom was a drama queen long before the term came out. Just about every day she would say, "I've never been so sick in my life." Okay, so I hear it over and over and I usually jumped to find out what was wrong, etc. So, one day she's sitting on the front porch and says, "I've never been so sick in my life." I evidently was *not* in a good mood and replied, "Then call a Doctor! What do I look like, a Doctor?" and I went to work. I get a call.

"Hello. Is this Kerry?"

"Yes, who are you?"

"This is the Lakewood Police Department, we have your mother."

"And what did she do?" I laughed. He didn't.

"You don't understand, we took her to Lakewood Hospital, she's in a diabetic coma."

For crying out loud! Are you kidding me!? The first time I don't jump it's for real. I couldn't believe it. I was sure he was telling me the truth; after all, he did have my mother. She was in the hospital and they were able to get her back and she was fine. Okay, so sometimes we may overreact and not jump. For the most part that's okay.

Sometimes we get guilt confused with remorse. I believe there is a place for the honest emotion we call remorse. The difference between guilt and remorse is that remorse has the element of a willingness to change oneself; guilt does not. They are two very different emotions, and once you understand the difference you too shall no longer be booked on any guilt trips.

I have had my fair share of feeling unsettled about what I was thinking sometimes. I don't know that I would call it guilt. There was a time when I was driving home from work after a 3-11PM shift that went later than expected. It was winter, cold, snowy and the streets and highway were isolated. As the snowflakes landed on the car windshield the wipers swayed to their own beat. It was quiet with the exception of the occasional snow plow passing by. I felt like I just wanted to keep on driving. There was no place in particular I wanted to go; I just didn't want to go home that night. As I drove in the snow on the highway I felt like my car was on autopilot. It just seemed to know where to go. It was mindless driving on my part. My mind was elsewhere. My mind was swirling like the snowflakes, only my thoughts were very troubling to me. I loved Jack more than anything, but I didn't want to go home. I was tired, it was late, and I felt I had been in this horrible situation of dealing with cancer way too long. If the truth be told, and this is the truth, I wanted it to be over. I wanted Jack's pain to stop. I wanted my head to stop feeling like it was going to explode any minute, and I wanted it all to be over. Right then and there I wanted this ended. As the tears flowed and I literally yelled at God, I thought I would go crazy if I had to deal with this one more day. I sat at the end of the exit ramp. The light was red and time stood still for a moment. I pulled myself together and drove home and hugged Jack as he slept. Well, it was longer than one more day after that night; it was a few more years in fact. I tell you this story because we're all human and we all have emotions. I didn't do this whole 'my husband is dying' thing perfectly. No one does. It is what it is. We get tired, we get angry, we feel bad, and we move on. We deal with our emotions the best we can. It's what I call compassion fatigue. We get fatigued, it *is* daunting, but we can get through it. And guilt does not have to be a part of it. There are enough people in the world who have opinions about what we should and shouldn't do. What we should and shouldn't say. We need to learn to take care of ourselves so that we can live with as much gratitude and grace as we can. It's not easy. Taking care of people who are dying on a daily basis as a professional, or not a professional, is difficult and emotional. You feel for them, and they feel for you as well. Jack's biggest worry was that he would be a burden to me and his family. He was never a burden. We loved him, and when you love someone as much as we loved Jack there is no way he could be a burden to anyone. I have often said that I would repeat those fourteen years all over again if I could just have him back, just to hold him one more time. I can't, and neither can any of us. What we can do is take it one day at a time, one step at a time and we will be okay.

On Fear - There are a lot of emotions we deal with and I would like to go through a few of the ones I experienced myself. A big one is fear. I believe that of all of them fear is the most difficult to deal with. It often deals with the unknown. We want to know what's ahead of us. Fear is a powerful emotion. Most people experience some fear throughout their lives, but it can feel heavier when we are in grief. There is a lot of fear around death no doubt. Fear of the unknown starts to settle in. Death at times can be confusing, especially to children who don't understand it. It's difficult for adults to understand it sometimes.

I believe most people have some sort of belief of where our Soul goes when we die. That life force inside of you that makes you, well, *you*. The Afterlife means different things to different people. Some people believe in it, some do not. Some of us believe in Heaven and Hell. Some believe in Karma. I have learned to respect what others believe. I have had a lot of experience in difficult situations where people have struggled to reconcile in their mind what they believe. Often we may question what and why we believe what we do. I know that I have. I have been able to support other people who have gone through, or are going through a great loss even if I don't share their same beliefs. What I try to share is the human understanding and willingness to be there to help someone else through the process. We live in a culture that is more accepting of other religions now than it previously had been. I think we speak a little more freely about it than people did when I was growing up. We see more interfaith and intercultural marriages. I learned a lot about different faiths and religious beliefs, about death and dying and where people believe Souls go during the eight years I worked as a Hospice Nurse. I absolutely loved it! Not to say it wasn't a hard job, it was. I found that there was nothing more sacred to me than helping someone transition from this life to the next. It was such a spiritual experience for me. It was an honor and a privilege to be able to be a part of that process every single time. I cannot even count the number of times I have witnessed such an event. It is priceless. Many people are afraid of death, I am not. I don't think I have ever been afraid of it. I have feared living at times more than death. Having been graced with the opportunity to see so many different faiths in action at such difficult times gave me a hope that stayed with me when I needed it in my own life when Jack died. I have seen some very peaceful deaths and I have seen some people struggle with death. I have been with families that have been calm and some that have been frantic. People handle death differently, and however we handle it is okay.

To all of the hospice families I have been so honored to have known, let me take this moment, as I reflect again on what you so graciously allowed me to share with you, the passing of your loved one. Such an intimate moment filled with love and joy and grief. I wish to thank you for the gifts you have given me. You have blessed me more than you could know.

I would like to share with you the most beautiful and emotional experience I have ever witnessed. I wasn't really sure about this at first, but the more I thought about it, the more I realize what a gift this man was not only to me, but to everyone around him. These were Jack's last moments with me.

I will say this, for being a hospice nurse, and pretty much knowing the signs when someone is going to die, I did not expect Jack to die on that day whatsoever. If there were any signs at all I totally missed them. For that I am grateful. He was up walking around, laughing, talking and eating small amounts of food. Skip his son had been over earlier in the day and they talked for quite some time. Their conversation was private, I was in my study. I know that Skip had said that his Dad had said to him, "I've got this..." with a thumb up sign during their conversation. A few of his friends came over around noon and they talked for a while, they laughed, they had fun. Jack asked me to make him some coffee, which I did and then promptly spilled on him when I tripped over the bedside table in the middle of the living room. He laughed and said, "You're going to kill me before this cancer does!" We laughed, he hugged me and gave me a kiss and said he wanted to lay down and take a nap on the hospital bed which had just been delivered in the living room.

Jack laid down on the bed and said, "Ha! This is pretty comfortable! Why didn't I let you order one of these for me before?!" He smiled that big smile at me. I absolutely loved his sense of humor. We laughed. He wouldn't let me order a hospital bed because he felt it made the house look like sick bay in the navy. I laid down on the sofa recliner. It was about 2PM. Diane, Skip's wife had texted me saying that our grandson Lee wanted to come over after school about 4PM to see Jack. I texted back that it would be fine. We fell asleep.

I heard someone talking; I thought Jack was asking me a question.

"Jack?" I waited a moment. I looked over..."Jack, sweetheart, do you need something?"

"I hope I did everything right." He said softly.

"What? Jack, are you okay?" I felt a little anxious as I looked over and Jack was simply laying there with his hands folded in a praying position with his eyes closed.

"I hope I did everything right. I pray that everything will be okay. Please forgive me for everything I did wrong. I hope it will now all be okay. Amen."

I realized at that moment he was saying a prayer. I slowly got up. I quietly walked around the bottom of the bed to the other side. He must have taken the oxygen off when he laid down. He was still. He didn't move. His hands were now by his sides.

"Jack?" He didn't answer. I hesitated for a brief moment as panic started to set in.

"Jack!" I grabbed him and hugged him. I knew he was gone. I gently kissed him goodbye.

It was our last moment together. I truly believe he woke me up to hear his last prayer. It was the most beautiful death I have experienced. It was peaceful; he did not struggle. He woke me, he shared his prayer with me and God and his soul left. It was amazing. I could not have asked for more. If there were signs that he was going to die that day I was blessed to have missed them. It happened the way it should have. I share this with you because not all deaths are horrendous. Fear of death doesn't have to overtake you. Death can be, and often is, very peaceful. This was, I would have to say, exceptional. I don't recall anyone ever saying a prayer and leaving when I was in the room, but I'm grateful it happened this way for us. I will always treasure these last few precious moments I was so divinely given in the sacred space of my heart.

I was grateful that Jack woke me to share his last prayer with him. It is a moment and a prayer I shall never forget. It was an honor and a privilege to be with this man who loved me more than anyone ever has, to share in his transition from this life to the next. It was a gift from both Jack and God to me. With gratitude and grace I thank them both.

I practiced hospice nursing for several years. I loved being a Hospice Nurse, and although Jack was not my patient, he was on Hospice when he died. I have been with a lot of people who have transitioned from this life to the next. I have always felt it both and honor and a privilege to be there at that time. It is a time when families are at their most vulnerable point, their grief is raw and you are a witness to the sacred. Life is sacred, whether it is the beginning or the end. It's all sacred. To be there, in the midst of it, is incredible.

> *'I feel I am in the realm of the mystical at times. Sleep does not come easy, if at all, some nights. I crave sleep like chocolate after pizza. I want to escape from the fear, but I can't. Jack's impending death leaves me aimless at times with an unsettling fear. I both wander and wonder what my life will be like. I can't imagine it; I don't want to imagine it. It only makes it more real and I am not quite ready for that reality. Are any of us really ready for it when it comes? I think not. I am afraid to look into the future and I am afraid if I don't I will be sorry later that I didn't do some of the things I could have when I had a more clear head about me. I am sure there are more pressing things to do right now than worry about the future. Maybe not.'*

I wrote those words after Jack had already gone through three cancer surgeries and open heart surgery and now facing chemotherapy. I was so afraid. Fear is such a scary thing. Fear is not a fact; it is however, an emotion. It's a very powerful emotion that can rule our lives if we let it. Fear can also ruin your life if you let it. It can destroy everything good you still have left in your life to live for. There is such a thing as a healthy fear. That's not what I am talking about. I am talking about a fear that can engulf you emotionally little by little until you are so overwhelmed with it you cannot make a decision because you are afraid it will be the wrong one. That's a paralyzing fear. It's a horrible place to be.

There are decisions that your loved one will have to make on their own. They may not be the decisions you would have made for yourself. It doesn't matter. No matter how hard it is, try to support that decision in the best way you know how. My husband made decisions about his health care that I would not have made about mine. We talked about things, a lot of things. We talked just about everything in fact.

Jack talked about his fear. He was not afraid of death. That was not one of his fears. His biggest fear was that he would not live long enough to see all his grandchildren graduate from high school. He did not. He missed the four youngest ones. His grandchildren were the world to him. No matter how he felt, if he could get there, he was at a team sporting event for all of them. He loved sports and he loved them. We went to Friday night football games even if his grandchildren weren't playing. He loved the atmosphere of kids and sports. He loved life.

Jack loved life. He would have given everything he had, and he did, to increase his chances of living a longer one. He amazed me. He gave more to life and love and people than anyone I know. He was a humble man with a huge heart. I should have such humility.

On Anger - Anger is also at the top of the list. Anger is a volatile emotion. The thing about anger is that something very simple can trigger it. Sometimes you don't even consciously know what triggered it. But there it is as big as life. It's not unusual to be angry at the person who has died. You may feel angry because you feel abandoned. I was. I was angry because I felt Jack left me. He had always been there for me. Now I didn't know what to do. Now the one person who validated my life on a daily basis was gone. Not only was I angry I was scared. I realized after I thought about it that I wasn't really angry with Jack, I was angry and the disease itself. The disease was robbed me of the man I loved more than anything. It was a resentment of sorts. I was angry because his death affected a lot of areas in my life. It felt personal even though it wasn't. It triggered my fear of abandonment. I had already lost a lot of significant people in my life. It triggered my fear of financial insecurity. How was I going to make it on my own, never having been on my own? Most of all I was angry that he was no longer here to share our lives together. There's a proverb that says: "Be slow to anger..." It doesn't say don't *get* angry, it just says to be slow about it. Being angry at what's going on around you is expected. You may find yourself angry with the people around you. You can be angry at God if you want to, you won't be the first. You can be angry at the whole disease process you are going through or have just been through. You may also be angry with yourself because you feel inadequate to handle what's right in front of you some days. It's normal.

How you release the anger is key. My suggestion would be to *release* it not *unleash* it. There's a difference. There's such a thing as clearing the air, *not* the room. Ask yourself what one thing can I do right now to release some of the anger? Maybe you can take a walk or a run to release some of the pent up emotion. Prayer and meditation, not medication, helps. It's been said that thoughts are prayers. Pray the Rosary or use Prayer Beads if you can. A short prayer is as good as a long one. Prayer is prayer. Now, about meditation. It's not all candles and Guru's. Really, it's not. Okay, I have to say that I do light a candle, but you don't have to! It's just there to keep me focused. You just sit down in a chair, close your eyes and start to relax. Breathe in and out slowly for a few breaths. Listen to your breathing, it's calming. You can focus on a word such as peace. It can be a phrase also such as "Peace be still" or "I am calm" or whatever phrase you want to use. Just try to keep it simple. Do it for maybe a minute or two and see how you feel. It takes practice to try not to let other thoughts interfere. If a thought that's unrelated floats through your mind don't worry, just focus again on your word or phrase. Do it as often as is necessary, it does help.

On Faith - To be honest this is a difficult topic for me to write about. I usually don't even *talk* about it. There was a time; to be sure, that I felt nothing could rock my faith. I was wrong. When I was a teenager I had a faith in something, I just wasn't sure what it was. God was confusing to me and I felt it was an all hell, fire and brimstone kind of thing. I have learned it is not. God *is not* the God my mother said he was, which is a good thing! It's amazing what we pick up in life on the way to growing up. I know for me my idea of God has changed several times over the years. I'm sure it will change again. One thing I do know is that God is consistent even if I am not. The sun still rises every morning and sets every evening and the moon rises every evening just the same. The rivers flow, the oceans roar and the stars are quiet at night. The seasons come and go every year just like clockwork. I am not anywhere near this consistent in my own life.

I have been angry *at* God, scared *of* God and at one point said to God: "I'm not talking to you and you know why!" God seems to be able to rise above my irritations with him, and my need to be angry, or just pouting because I felt betrayed by him. His plans clearly were not my plans at times. I had a difficult time reconciling the two.

There were times I was *at* church, not *in* church so to speak. I have for years sat in a pew at church half listening to a Sermon wondering what the heck I was doing there. I somehow go back at times trying to deepen my Spiritual life. Jack worked at the church for about ten years, and I went with him to Church. I have struggled to make sense out of a lot of it. People at church are great people: open, warm, and caring. I just didn't get what I felt *they* got somehow. God has, at times, felt close to me, other times not so much. So you can see the difficulty here when I was trying to hang onto some sort of faith when things turned from good to bad and bad to worse.

When Jack had open heart surgery it was about four and a half years after they had removed the lower lobe of his left lung. All seemed well as he was in the operating room and recovery. When he was out of surgery I was called to the Surgeon's office. My friend Rini Blakemore was with me the entire day. She got there about 7 am and now it was almost 7 pm. Rini has a faith that I believe is unshakeable. She was going to leave, I told her to go home, it was getting late and Jack was fine he was in Recovery. She decided to stay.

I met the Surgeon in his office.

"Well, the surgery went well. The surgery was successful" he said.

"And?" I said as I looked at him sitting across from me in a large black leather chair behind his desk.

"His lung cancer is back" he said hesitantly looking at

me for some sort of reaction. He clearly was uneasy with this.

"What? Oh my god. Did you know this before you went in?" I could barely get the words out.

"Yes, we did."

"Does Jack know? Does *anybody* know?"

"You know."

I took a very deep breath. The tears started flowing, and I was scared. More scared than I had ever been. My world felt like it was slowly shattering as I sat there.

"Okay... I have only one question. Just one and I need a really good answer because I just can't understand this. Why in the world would you do open heart on a man whose cancer has returned? It makes no sense. He's going to die and you put him through all of this?"

"If we didn't fix his aortic valve, and it closed, nothing else would have mattered. We had to fix his heart in order for him to be here for us to be able to fix the cancer." He was gentle with his answer.

"Okay. I can live with that." It at least made some sense. He was right; if the valve closed he would have been gone.

"When are you going to tell him?"

"After he gets out of ICU. We don't want to put any more stress on his body than he already has right now."

Talk about sitting on a time bomb. I left the office feeling like my feet never touched the floor. I felt like this was all a very bad dream and I couldn't wake up. I was walking toward the lobby where Rini was. I just couldn't keep it in.

"What's the matter? Is Jack okay?"

"Rini, Jack's lung cancer is back. I don't know what to do. He doesn't know, they aren't going to tell him until he's out of ICU. I can't believe this is happening" the words trailed out of my mouth. I just stood there and cried.

"What about his kids? Are you going to tell them?"

"I can't. I can't tell them before he knows. He has a right to know first. They're all up there outside of ICU and I have to go in there and act like everything's fine. I don't know if I can do it."

"Just stay calm and I'll go with you to ICU and let's just go from there."

We went up to ICU and Jack had just been brought in from recovery.

"How's my dad?" asked Shari, his oldest daughter.

"He's good, everything went fine."

"No cancer right? They didn't find any more cancer when they were in there did they?" She looked directly at me. She had been so anxious and so afraid that they would.

"No, no cancer. He's fine." I lied. Just as I said it Rini put her hand on my back, as if to say, 'go ahead and tell them', I couldn't.

I felt so betrayed by God at that point. I walked Rini down the hall, and said "I can't do this. I cannot believe God could do this to him again. I'm losing my faith Rini, I can't even pray right now."

"Kerry, we'll pray *for* you until you can pray for yourself. It's going to be okay." She was the only person who knew right then. I could not have had a better friend by my side when this happened. She had faith where I did not. To tell me that she and my friends would pray for me until I could pray for myself was amazing.

I did not pray that night. I was angry, sad, and scared. I didn't sleep much either. I called my daughter Candy in Seattle first and told her what happened. She too has an incredible faith.

"Do you want to say a prayer?" she asked gently.

"No. You pray. I'll listen." I could not keep the tears

from flowing. I felt like my heart was breaking. She prayed. I listened.

"Mom, it's gonna be okay."

Well, it wasn't exactly okay but I had to pull myself together enough to be able to have a conversation with Jack and not let on that I knew something was seriously wrong. It was tough because Jack could always tell when something was wrong.

A few days after Jack was out of ICU and in a Step Down unit I started getting really antsy. He still didn't know. I wasn't sure if I should tell him or not. I called his friend Bob Kazy and asked him if he could come down to the Clinic in about an hour.

"Sure, what's up?"

"Jack's lung cancer is back and he doesn't know it and they haven't told him yet. I'm going to tell him and I'd like you to be there after I do. He's going to need someone to talk to and I know he talks to you about this."

"I'll be there. How are you holding up?"

"I'm not. I just need to do this. I've been sitting on it four days now, lying to his kids, telling everyone he's fine and he's not."

"Okay, I'll be there in about an hour."

I went to Jack's room and they had just taken out the five chest tubes he had in from surgery. I sat on the side of his bed, held his hand and tried to hold back the tears.

"What" he said. He knew something was going on.

"Sweetheart, your lung cancer is back."

"What? No, they said everything was fine!"

"Everything was fine with the open heart true, but not everything is fine."

"What next..." tears filled his eyes.

I have only seen Jack with tears in his eyes twice in twenty six years. The first time was when they first told him he had cancer. The second time was when I told him that the cancer was back.

"Bob Kazy is coming down. I called him and told him I was going to tell you."

"Okay, good."

"Does anybody else know?"

"Rini and Candy know. I also called Tom Madden." Tom was our Pastor.

"I didn't tell your kids. I thought you should know before everyone else knows. It's up to you to tell your kids when you think it's the right time."

"I can't tell them. I just can't. Can you tell them for me?"

"Of course I will. I'll do whatever you want."

"I don't know how we're going to get through this Jack. Here I am crying and you're the one with the cancer. I'm so sorry."

"Don't be. God will get us through this. He has before."

I agreed, but didn't really believe it. Jack had such a simple faith. God's in control and he'll take care of it. Always positive. I was far from there at this point.

I eventually got *some* faith back. I had to. I was not going to make it if I didn't. It was a slow, slow process. Two steps forward and three back. I questioned everything in my head. Was there a God? Where *is* this God? Why is he doing this to us? The questions in my head were endless. I came to the realization that God did not cause Jack's cancer, Jack got cancer. That simple. Easier said than done I'm sure. But in reality a lot of people die of cancer. I don't think God causes cancer any more than I believe he causes earthquakes, floods or hurricanes. They are an act of nature, not an act of God.

As I write this I am reliving painful parts of the past. In a way it seems to be a good thing. I can look at where I was and where I am right now. I have worked hard on trying to relate to God. I still get angry, sad, or mad. There are still some days where I pout and don't want to talk to him...at all. But I do. I say I'm angry, sad, or mad. I say what I feel. It helps. I don't think prayer changes God, I think that prayer changes *us*. I doubt that I'm alone in my search for answers as to who and/or what God is. It seems to be a part of the human condition.

By the time Jack was diagnosed the third time I pretty well knew that it was coming. So did Jack. After a chemotherapy session Jack said to me "I can't do this anymore. I don't know what we're going to do." I kissed him on the forehead and said, "We're going to handle this with gratitude and grace." It surprised even me when I said it. It had to come from somewhere, but I didn't have any thought of saying it at all. But I did and I meant it. We were dealing with a third bout of cancer now. There were not more options, it was the final stages. I knew Jack was secure in his faith, he pretty much always had been. What I realized was that somewhere I knew there was a God that would take care of all of this, and he did. That's not to say it was easy, it wasn't. What I learned to do was trust a little at a time, and when things started to fall apart, and Jack died four months later I knew I would somehow be okay.

It is all about gratitude and grace.

Plan B

*P*lan B started long before either of us knew we would really need it. It initially started when my husband's father had given us a copy of his funeral arrangements that were prepaid and everything we needed in the event of his death. We had moved to Florida to take care of him and he wanted to make sure everything was done and that we did not have anything to worry about. We thought it was such a great idea that we decided that we could do the same for our children in the event that something unfortunate should happen to both of us.

We were visiting family in Ohio and since we wanted to be buried in the same cemetery as my husband's mom and dad we went there. I have to admit, I was young, or so I felt in my early 40's, to be making funeral arrangements. It was surreal sitting in a funeral home picking out a headstone and deciding what you want it to say some forty five - fifty years ahead of time. Did we want flowers? Did I want a picture? No, pictures were absolutely out! I hate having my picture taken when I'm alive, I sure don't want it done when I'm dead. Ok, no pictures which leaves the flowers, sayings, designs, etc. Jack always signed everything with a little smiley face. He said he wanted a smiley face and since I collected rabbits I chose a bunny. We chose the saying, Always And Forever with gold roses on the corners. We laughed a bit nervously about it all, but when all was said and done, we were relieved. It had our names and the year of our births on it and blank spaces for the date of our deaths. We were done with the headstone. That I will say was a little nerve racking. The woman asked if we would like it placed now or put in storage until 'needed'. We both said at the same time, "put it in storage!"

I recall walking through the cemetery holding my husband's hand, feeling loved and very secure. It was peaceful. We chose out plot in the Prayer Garden, a quiet place far from the road. There is a beautiful wall arrangement of three granite angels in white with flowing wings looking upward to the sunlight. They fall into a beautiful blue background and at once I felt at peace just looking at them. I knew it would all be okay if we were there someday, not today. I had no idea that someday would come sooner than we had both expected.

We took advantage of the payment plan and paid minimal payments on a five year plan. I will say, when the last payment was made, I was somehow oddly relieved. The Deed followed in the mail, along with the outline of the items purchased etc. and I put them away in a safe place with the Wills.

Ah, the Wills. Wills are something just about everyone, unless you're rich and famous, and we were not, don't really like to think about. But the true question regarding the Will comes down to one very simple question: "Do you want your spouse and children or the Government to get what belonged to you?" That's the question plain and simple. Trust me, the Government, State, City or any other taxing agency would love to have it, no matter how big or small the amount. That's not where it should go.

I'm sure you, as I, would want your spouse or children to have whatever is in your Estate. If you also want a portion of your Estate to go to charity along with your family then my suggestion is to put it into the Will.

As we say in nursing, "If it isn't written, it didn't happen." If you just *said* you wanted a certain amount to go to charity, or your brother or sister if you don't have children, it does not matter. When Jack and I did our Wills, I put in mine that no matter where I move to, and yes, I moved across the country from Ohio to Washington State, that I will be buried next to him, no matter what happens. That 'no matter what happens' includes should I marry again, which I have no plans to do. And he will need to be one very understanding man if I ever do. If the shoe were on the other foot, I would respect the same and carry out someone else's wishes to do the same. Just because someone dies it does not mean that you give up what meant so much to both of you. If you decided together to be buried together my feeling is that others will need to understand and respect you and your wishes. If it is in your Will it cannot be changed by anyone but you. Yes, Wills can be very emotional, trust me. It is also a huge relief once you have done it. Whether you are ill or not, accidents happen every day that we never plan on. You can hire an Attorney or find a Will online or at a Staples etc. just fill it out and have it Notarized.

Plan B doesn't come without a Budget to think about. Now, I will tell you it is not easy to sit down and think about living alone, let alone planning a Budget for one. I know, because I did it. However, it is not the worst thing in the world. A worse thing would be that you end up alone and have no idea what to do and what you have to live on. You may agree that could be worse than at least attempting to have a general idea. I said a general idea.

This is not written in stone by any means. This is just a thought to give you some idea of what you may need. It may also give you some much needed peace of mind, which it did in my case. I was terrified to even think about doing this at first. Here's what happened.

I took the advice of my sister, Kathy who had said to me when Jack was first diagnosed, "Step into the future, look around and then come back out. But you have to come back out." I had done that many times since his first diagnosis through the third, and often for all the years we went through all of it. Those words have served me well as I trust they will you.

When I decided to sit down and do this, I did it a little at a time. I literally walked into the future and saw myself living by myself. YES, I was scared. Yes, I started to cry, and no, I was not sure that I could do it. The first time I looked at it I just wrote a list of Needs. Now, I have come to realize that Needs and Wants on my list were two very different things! I *need* basic necessities; I *wanted* a few additional things. Okay, probably more than a few. However, I stuck with the necessities. We were, at the time, living in a home which I knew I would not be keeping. It was too large for me, and I knew we would soon be downsizing due to the medical bills which were getting very large at this point. So, I did some research online for the price of (1) bedroom apartments. I decided not to make any rash moves, such as buying a house, etc. for at least one year. I also had made plans to move to the Seattle area to be close to my daughter and her family earlier. But I still needed to plan the price of an apartment to rent. I included the basics, Utilities, Cell Phone, Food, Gas for the car, Car Insurance, Health Insurance. This was my first rough draft, my step into the future and walking back out. I put it away for a while.

Now, you have to understand my husband Jack had the best sense of humor I've ever seen. About four years after my first rough draft of my Budget, we were at Cleveland Clinic in the waiting room of the doctor's office. It's relatively quiet; obviously, we're at the Taussig Cancer Center. Not a lot of chatter going on there, it's a really somber place sometimes. I discreetly pull out my little notebook and pen and start writing. Now, I did a lot of jotting down notes wherever I was so this was not unusual.

"What are you doing?" Jack said as he looked up from reading a magazine.

"Budget for One..." I sighed and then I laughed.

"Well! You better sure as hell put hair and nails first! God only knows that comes before anything else!" he said a little louder than he thought he did.

I tried hard not to laugh out loud but I just couldn't keep it in. I laughed so much I thought I was going to cry! Patients around us who heard him just looked at us. We tried to stop laughing for a few minutes but we couldn't. It doesn't have to be all serious all the time. If it is, you're in for a long, long road. No, illness is not a funny thing, but humor takes the edge off sometimes. Sometimes there are a lot of edges; but if we can smooth some of them with a bit of humor we will get through it a little better. We will also have those funny memories to think about later and smile once again.

So, my experience has also been that that there are men *and* women who have no idea whatsoever how to write a check or pay the bills or what the bills even are. Some people still write checks, and some pay them online. Often they are debited from our checking accounts each month. Do you know how and where the bills are paid from? If you do, great! If you don't, well, that's okay too because I have a few simple suggestions for you.

I have heard there is such a thing as a Love Box. Now, this is new to me, but it makes a lot of sense! It can be a literal box, or a desk drawer, or an envelope in the safe. The Love Box is a place where important items are placed so that both of you know where they are. This is very important. Items kept there are the Wills, insurance policies, important phone numbers, bank records, investment account information, computer passwords, etc. Allow yourself the time to set this up if you don't already have this.

I cannot stress this enough. If you do all your banking online and your spouse has no idea how to use a computer, as did mine, they need the passwords so that someone they trust can access this information. My husband hated computers. He could send email if he had to and forget the rest. I paid all of our bills online, but I had a list of all the bills and which accounts they were paid from along with the passwords. Had I not done this and something happened to me first he would have been totally lost. At the time of great loss people are stressed enough. Not knowing how much money you have at your disposal and what bills are being paid and where you stand is one nightmare you do not need added to what you are already going through! Yes, there will always be people who don't want to learn computers, and that's fine. We don't have to insist they do it our way, just let them know where the information is and they can get someone to help them from there.

Jack and I had a joint checking and savings account and I had an individual checking account as well. This was one of the first things I did on my Plan B. I remember walking into the bank and setting up a checking account in my name. It had been a long time since I had an individual account. It felt odd. Sad, I would say more than odd, but necessary. The woman said to me, evidently seeing my wedding rings:

"Will your husband be on this account as well?"

"No, I'm setting up this account as part of my Plan B. My husband has lung cancer and I'm smart enough to know that I need a Plan B and I don't want to have to deal with closing accounts in both our names and opening a single account in my name when he dies. I will have enough stress to deal with and this will be one less thing I have to do then..." I remember my words trailing off as I tried not to make eye contact.

"Wow, I'm really sorry. But that's a really smart idea you know. Most women don't think that way. What a good idea not to have to deal with all that stress later."

"Right, I will have to close the other accounts but that's all I will have to do is close them. Everything else will already be done. I will have my payroll deposited to this account and be paying some of our bills from this one and others from the joint one."

"Okay, we can do that for you!" She said with a smile, and it was done.

I was relieved. I felt sad when I left the bank. I can still see myself walking across the asphalt parking lot with the faded white striping with tears in my eyes as I went to my car. I took a deep breath and got in my car. I sat there for a minute and then I cried. I was full of fear. Fear of the future, fear of losing my best friend, the love of my life and of being on my own. I always prided myself on being independent, yet at this very moment it was the *last* thing I wanted. I didn't want to be independent from Jack right now. I wanted him to be here forever. I knew it wasn't going to be possible, but it was what I wanted. I sat there and cried for a good fifteen minutes then I was okay. I had let the stress out. I knew I did what I had to do, and that Jack was at home, safe and sound at the moment. I was okay. I went home.

For a couple who never stopped talking from Cleveland to Florida in a car on road trips you would think we would have covered everything under the sun. Well, we pretty much did, except a few very important things. I can tell you that Jack had a very difficult time talking about his cancer, not just at the beginning, but anytime. I can also tell you that of all the seeming millions of conversations we had over just about everything we rarely discussed it. It drove me crazy! I can count on one hand the times we sat down and had a serious conversation about it. It was probably three. Three times in fourteen years. I am very serious when I say this. I think part of the problem was that we were so close that we were both afraid of hurting each other. Jack had mentioned a few times that he felt like a burden. I tried several times to reassure him that he was not a burden, and that I loved him more than life itself. It didn't matter. He felt what he felt and I wasn't able to change that. He held me when I said nothing but just started crying in the middle of the night when I thought he was asleep. Sometimes there are no words. There are only feelings that can't be verbally expressed. That's okay. There comes a time that you do have to talk about some things. Specifically the thing I called the elephant in the room.

That's not to say we didn't discuss things that needed to be discussed like Life Insurance and where I would move to or funeral arrangements. We did, but that too, was minimal, and they were quick conversations. It was difficult. It was painful and it hurt. I know I was deeply affected by it and he just would not talk about it. I was very upset about it, and so I went to talk with our Pastor, Tom

Madden, who knew both of us well. The conversation went something like this:

"Tom, Jack won't even talk to me about his cancer and it's driving me nuts!"

"Okay, what won't he talk about?"

"He won't tell me anything!"

"Like what? What do you want him to tell you?"

"I don't know, just anything! Something!"

Okay, so you can see where this conversation was going. I am now stressed to the max and ready to rip a Preacher's head off! And a Preacher I think the world of no less!

"Come on Tom! This isn't funny! He won't even *talk* about it. Nothing! It's the elephant in the room for god's sake!"

"Tell me, exactly what *is it* you want him to say?" he said a little exasperated as he leans back into his chair and gives me the questioning eye look. "What words do you want to hear?"

"I don't know," then as I try to hold back the tears, "I just want him to talk to someone. I don't care if it's not me. I just want him to talk to *someone!* No one can go through this alone Tom. I know he can't talk to me or he would. I know that. But he can't keep this inside. He can't."

"He talks to me" he said softly, and he smiled.

Then I was okay. Tom I trusted with my life. He had been there with us from the start. He married us. He was with us through some pretty rough times with kids, the surgeries, my faith, and major lack of it many times. Tom has always been a rock for us. I knew Jack was in good hands. There were a few other men in Jack's life that he talked with and I was okay with that. He had his confidants and I had mine. You see, sometimes we can't be the person they can talk to about everything, as much as we may want it to be. Jack often felt that somehow it was his fault that he got cancer, which I felt was ridiculous to start with. He had a very rare cancer, which had two different types of cancer cells in the same tumors. It was tough to treat, and when it came back it came back with a vengeance. He held deeply that my emotional pain and suffering was his fault. It was not. It was just part of the process.

When I thought about it I realized that I too did not tell Jack how I felt about everything. I called Tom when his cancer came back the second time and cried and cried. In that sense we were two of a kind. I had some very special women in my life, and I still do, that saw both of us through thick and thin. We knew when we could broach something and when we couldn't. When we couldn't I think we each intuitively knew it and we talked it over with someone who knew us and the situation.

There was the Elephant In The Room Scenario which included a conversation that I felt needed to happen that just wasn't happening. Of course, when I think it should happen, and have a husband that doesn't really want to talk, well, that becomes a question of timing. Sometimes timing is everything. There were times I could talk about Jack's cancer and there were times I could not. He obviously was the same. It wasn't that either of us was in denial, but, it was just so heavy on us emotionally. When we thought it was gone and it came back again, well, it was just too much for either of us. After having a reprieve of four and a half years and its return and surgery and chemo, well, it was time to talk.

We were now living in an apartment home and Jack had finished chemo. It was a Sunday morning and we were sitting at the small dining area table. We were drinking coffee, and I had such an uneasy feeling in my stomach.

"Jack, we need to talk about the elephant in the room."

"What elephant?" He said as he looked behind him toward the living room. He was serious.

"Are you kidding me?" I just looked at him. Is he really looking for an elephant?!

"What are you talking about Kerry? I have no idea what you're talking about."

"Okay," I took a deep breath, "how about we talk about what's going to happen to me when something happens to you? Where am I going to be? What am I going to do? That's the elephant in the room we never talk about."

"Oh, that. Yeah that..." he looked sad as he looked into my eyes.

"I'm going to be fine, I am." I interrupted, "I'm going to Candy's in Seattle, and I'm not living with Candy, just moving to that area. I just want you to know that I will be okay. There's nothing here for me anymore after you're gone. I need to be by my family, whatever there is of it. She and Doug and the kids are it. They *are* my family, at least the ones that stay put. " The tears started.

"I am so glad you said that," he said as he slowly got up from the table and walked over to me.

"I've been worried about you and what you were going to do. Seattle is where you belong...with Candy and Doug and the kids. They are your family, and those kids need their Gramma to be close by. I am so relieved." He hugged me as I stood up.

"I know this is tough to talk about Jack, but you have to know I'll be okay. I *need* you to know that in the end I too, will be okay. As difficult as this is, it needs to be said. It's all part of Plan B."

"Plan B? What's Plan B?" he looked at me a little funny. He evidently put it out of his thoughts.

"Well, it's like this: We are living in Plan A: Life as it is right now. Plan B is my life without you. I am smart enough to know that I will need Plan B, and there are things I have to do now that will make it easier to get through the rough times when they come. Plan B is that piece of it. We did our Will's years ago; we bought our cemetery plots, made arrangements, etc. We know where the insurance policies are. The bills are in order, well, sort of. And my plan to move to Seattle is part of Plan B. It's something I don't have to worry about, it's already been decided and I don't have to worry about it anymore. It's not something I think about every day, it's just there when I need it. If I think about something I need to add to it I write it down. That's Plan B in a nutshell."

"I remember now - I love you!" he said as he hugged me so tight and I cried.

I was glad to be able to talk to him about Plan B. Not that it was a secret, it wasn't. It just isn't something easy to share with someone who's dying. On the other hand, it may be a good thing to share when you can find the right moment, as we did, to let them know that you *will* be okay. Not that you will be out dancing in the streets, but that you will be okay and have a plan. You are not going to fall on your face. You will have problems adjusting, we all do, but you will adjust your Plan B and you will make it, because you have somewhere to start from. The beauty of Plan B is that it can always be adjusted.

Talk to someone you trust. Talk to someone who will listen, not someone who is multitasking while you are pouring your heart out! You laugh! Trust me, they're around! If you can get away for a cup of coffee or tea or take a walk. Not a jog! You're talking here, we're worrying about your *heart* - not your health! My good friend Rini and I went for ice cream and walked through the park. When she's not doing that she runs half-marathons. She never trained for marathons *while* we were talking. She was present and in the moment. Her being present and in the moment with me on so many occasions meant more to me than anyone will ever know. She literally saved my sanity at times. If you have a friend or friends like that you are blessed. And when you have the chance to be that 'listening friend' for someone else please do it like my friend Rini did it for me.

This is the kind of friend Rini is. When Jack went in for open heart surgery at Cleveland Clinic it was supposed to be for an Aortic valve replacement surgery and one bypass. We arrived at the Clinic at 6 AM and Rini met us there shortly after. Surgery was scheduled for 9 AM. Everyone was anxious but given where we were, I felt reasonably okay. I stayed with Jack as long as they would let me until they took him in to prep him for the surgery. We said good-bye in the hallway, I kissed him, smiled and told him he still looked fantastic with his green cap on his head and we laughed.

I went down to the waiting area. Family members were ushered into a room and explained what to expect while our loved ones were in surgery. They would update us every few hours, we could watch the monitor board with the initials and know where he was, etc. We were told that we would be notified when the patient was being put on the heart lung bypass machine and when they were taken off the heart lung bypass machine. They said they would tell us when the patient went into the recovery room and the surgeon would either call the desk and would talk to us, or he would change and be in his office and we would be told to go to the office. We were assured that if we were called to the office it did not mean that there were any problems, only that some of the Surgeons liked to talk to family members in their office rather than on the phone. We were also instructed on what to expect when the patient went home, and given an opportunity to ask questions. It was all very organized.

After going out to the waiting room, I found Rini and we went to the Cafe for coffee. We did the usual idle chit chat, looked through some magazines and watched some mindless TV in between conversations.

"Are you nervous?" she asked, with her 'you better tell me the truth' look in her eyes.

"No. Not really. He's been through worse already." I said casually.

"I know, but this *is* open heart girl!"

"Yeah, I know. He's in the best hands he could be in! The head of open heart is in there with him! Can't ask for more than that."

A few hours passed, we were told he was on the heart lung machine. I wasn't too worried. We had lunch at the Cafe. We drank more coffee, then more coffee and time seemed to be going slower and slower.

"You think he's okay in there?" Rini said

"Of course he is! They would have called us if there was a problem. Remember?"

"Right"

Now it's been literally hours and I'm getting nervous and I start walking around. Pacing is a better word. I check at the desk. No one has an update for me. I can start to feel my own heart racing. Having worked in Cardiac I know a little too much, just enough to drive myself nuts with it.

I tell myself that he's been in there too long, and now I'm starting to be concerned.

"Okay Rini, now I'm worried..."

"Did they call you? I didn't hear it."

"No. I just think something's wrong. I think he's been on that heart lung bypass machine way too long. He should have been off of it a long time ago!"

"He's okay. They would have called you over there if he wasn't." She tried to reassure me.

A little while later I was called to the desk. Jack was off the heart lung bypass machine and doing fine. What a relief! Now I just needed to wait for them to finish the surgery and take him to recovery and then I could talk with the surgeon.

As we were waiting, there was a young man who kept coming over to us and asking if we needed anything. He had offered us coffee earlier and we said no thanks we were fine. Here he was again for about the third time.

"I think this guy is flirting with you!" she laughed.

"No he's not! He's young enough to be my son!"

He thinks you're hot! He keeps checking you out!" she looked at me and we both burst out laughing! "I'm telling Jack! Your poor husband is in there on a heart lung machine and you're out here flirting with someone who could be your son!"

"Rini!" I laughed, "Jack would love it! And besides, I'm not flirting with this guy! I have no idea who he is."

"Hey! Maybe he can tell us what's really going on with Jack. Want to ask him?"

"Are you kidding? We could get this poor kid in trouble Rini."

"Look, he's been smiling at you all day! Just ask, okay? What could it hurt?"

"Okay, I'll ask. But I'm telling Jack you made me do it."

So, I walk over to my smiling friend and tell him that we have been there all day and really would like to know if he could tell us anything. At first he hesitates. Rini is right behind me, literally on my heels, and I just ask if there was anything he could tell us we would really appreciate it, but not if it's going to get him in any trouble. He says it's not a problem and that he's not going to get into any trouble and starts clicking into the computer. He tells me that Jack has 'just been closed up', meaning that the wires are all in place in his chest and the chest tubes are in place and he is ready to go into the Recovery room. He said he was not allowed to read the notes to me but that Jack was stable and on his way. That was all I needed to know.

Shortly after that, the desk called me over and said the Surgeon would meet me in his office and gave me the room number of the office where I should meet him.

"Do you want me to go with you?"

"Oh, no. Rini, you have been here all day! You need to go home and get some rest. I'm just going to go over and see the surgeon and then go to ICU to see Jack when I leave there. I'm fine, really."

"No, I think I'll stay. Besides, it should only take a few minutes. Sounds like everything went well."

I've already shared what happened between the Surgeon and myself earlier. The point is that everybody needs a "Rini" in their life. Someone they trust and can talk to when the going gets rough.

Your Afterlife

*T*here is something that I call "Post Funeral Clean Up". After the last casserole has been delivered, and the last sympathy card received, it never fails that the calls start getting further in between and the visits of friends less frequent. I'm not sure if that comes from people assuming that you're okay now, or they just don't know what to do. After all, condolences were given at the funeral, flowers were sent along with a card. Now what? People often don't know what to say after that. It can be awkward for them. They're not sure if they should bring up the deceased in conversation for fear of making you feel bad, or saying what they feel might be the wrong thing. So often people who don't know what to do, do nothing. It's not their fault, they just don't know what to do or say. It seems to have all been said already.

Blended families can also be a touchy situation. People who say they will keep in touch sometimes don't. They mean well, but for whatever reason it just doesn't happen. It may feel hurtful but it's probably not intentional. People move on with their lives and some are still processing their own grief as best they can. When we don't see family members or hear from them it feels like the "out of sight, out of mind" scenario has kicked in. It doesn't have to be that way. Make the phone call yourself. Yes, pick up the phone and call them. Send a card yourself. In our current society everyone is so transient. People don't live close together anymore. A lot of families' live great distances apart to start with. If you get angry over it it's only going to add to your frustration and grief. You have enough to deal with.

If you come from a fractured family to start with that's difficult was well. I know that I had a family member that passed away that I was not close to at all. However, my sister who lived with her was. *I* needed to reach out to *her* and make sure *she* was doing okay. It had nothing to do with the person who died. It had to do with her. It was her loss and I needed to recognize that. It's the living that still need comforted. I need to be mindful of the fact that I am not the only one who has lost someone here. No matter how close the person is to *us*, others are grieving as well. It also helps to get out of myself and think about how someone else may be feeling and just check up on them. It doesn't have to be a long drawn out conversation. Just give them a quick call and ask how they're doing. We don't know what we don't know. And what I *do* know is that if I am feeling stuck in grief then I hope I have enough foresight to give someone else a call or send a card to that someone who is grieving as well. Sometimes, it's just not all about me. Or about me at all.

I wrote a little about fear earlier. I have feared living alone. I had never lived alone before. I feared living without Jack, I feared that loneliness that would engulf me. I have cringed at the very thought of waking up without him next to me. I bought a smaller bed so it doesn't seem so obvious that no one else is there. That may sound a bit odd, but I needed to have less space next to me so that I wasn't so focused on the empty space. For me there was nothing worse than one person in a King sized bed so I got rid of it.

So, what about *YOU*??? It's pretty much so far been all about the person who has the illness. Granted, in many ways it should be and often needs to be. However, I have a friend who is not a nurse who said to me years ago, "Kerry, if you took half as good of care of yourself as you do your patients you would be in fantastic shape!" She meant that mentally because physically I was in the best shape of my life I had ever been in. That too changed, when I didn't take such good care of myself. Then I had to make the effort to focus on my health once again. It probably would have been easier to stay doing the things I was doing to stay healthy at the time, but I didn't. I let other things get in the way. I don't mean Jack. I mean Jack's illness, worry, my job, finances, medical bills, not sleeping, not eating right and no exercise. Things I did on a regular basis before my life started changing in big ways and small. One by one they went by the wayside. If you can avoid doing that it will help you in the long run. I can't blame it on any one thing. I was the one who chose, consciously or unconsciously, not to focus on my health but on other things going on around me, and there were a lot of things going on around me. I'm happy to say that today I am more focused on being a healthier whole person. Do I do it perfectly? Absolutely not. I didn't do it perfectly before, what makes me think I'm going to do it perfectly now? I leave perfection to the gods; they're better equipped to handle it.

You *will* get through this. It will take time and there will be a transformation that takes place in your life. There is timing to transformation. Things have been, or presently are, in some cases changing. They will be changing sooner than you wished for in your life. Change is difficult for all of us, or so it seems. Think of how hard it is to change one little thing or habit in your life. It's hard. Now you are faced with changing not only little things in your life but huge things as well. Things you don't want to change. It's difficult, but it can be done with gratitude and grace. I only know that because I have seen many changes in my life over the years of dealing with my own personal losses. Change came whether I wanted it to or not; whether I was prepared for it or not. Some changes I was prepared for, some I was not. Change can be staggering if you aren't prepared. One thing is certain about change - it is inevitable.

My suggestion is that you not make any major changes, unless absolutely necessary, for the first year after your loss. I'm not talking about cleaning out a closet. I'm talking about moving, selling your home, or quitting your job because you just can't stand it one more moment. Those kinds of changes on top of grief will only compound your suffering. I would ask that you think about getting some outside professional help from either a Counselor that deals with grief and loss or join a support group such as GriefShare. GriefShare is a Christian based support group that has local chapters and meets on a weekly basis. Most churches have someone you can talk to along with your Minister or Priest. Not everyone is comfortable in a support group talking about grief. Grief is a highly charged emotional issue. I have noticed that more women than men attend these groups, but the men I have talked with are open and honest. They too have their feelings and need to share their burdens as well. I have used all of these options that were offered to me and they have all helped at some point or another.

I went to a weekly support group for a few months and talked with a Counselor. Sometimes I spoke with my therapist. I spoke with a therapist a lot over the years, and still do. I needed someone who understood what I was going through. Yes, I had my friends, and they were Jack's friends too. They too lost a great guy! Sometimes it was okay to talk about Jack to a good friend of ours because our friends could share their feelings as well. However, the deep down thoughts in my Soul, the words I could barely get out of my mouth and the fears that left me sleepless at night, I shared with my therapist. That, I did. And as I mentioned, I did it a lot! Jack would joke that I had David Ackerman, my therapist, on speed dial! I also spent some time doing meditation. It wasn't all a mystical kind of thing. I would light a candle and just sit down and try to clear my mind of all the random thoughts that were cluttering it up. I would try to focus on positive thoughts. Positive thoughts are not going to change the situation that we find ourselves in, but they can influence the way we react to the situation at hand. It's okay to do whatever it takes. It takes what it takes to get through this for each of us.

What will your life look like? It's okay to think about. I wouldn't dwell there too much, unless that's where you are right now and you *have* to think about it right now. I suggest you look at it in some small way. You don't want to get blindsided by it. Just don't get stuck there.

After Jack had his first lung surgery and I had a really severe cold that kept both of us up at night I decided to sleep in the guest bedroom for a week until I was over it. I was so afraid of compromising him and afraid he would get sick so I moved into the guest room. It was odd. Very odd. I remember sitting on a queen size bed in a beautiful comfortable room looking around as I drank a hot cup of tea and saying to myself, 'So this is what it looks like to be alone.' It was a random thought that just crossed my mind seemingly out of nowhere. No doubt it wasn't out of nowhere, but at the time it appeared to be. I sat there for a few moments and the tears started gently falling from my eyes. I didn't want to think about it. I hadn't slept alone, away from Jack for years, and here I am trying to keep him safe from getting a cold that could turn into Pneumonia for him, and I realize probably for the first time, what it may be like to be alone. It scared me. I didn't want to think about it. My head was already stuffy, and nothing like crying to make it worse! Although it was snowing outside, I was warm enough, but I reached for the comforter anyway and wrapped myself up in it. I just sat there for awhile, snuggled as it were, trying not to think. I let the tears flow and I sipped my tea and I calmed down. Reality was upon me in some small way. My mind was letting me know that there would be days like this to come and changes would be necessary, big and small. I needed to be willing to look at it. I was grateful that it was a small thing at the time. Bigger things came later, but not all at once. Changes can be subtle or harsh, but either way, change can be difficult if we let it. Or, we can try to prepare for some of it so that we will not be so tripped up by the small stuff so when the bigger changes come we aren't as devastated by them.

What about you? If you are already in what I call Your After Life there is a question out there that needs an answer. I also needed to answer it for myself: What do you want? What did I want? I had no idea what I wanted. I just knew that I didn't want what I had at the moment which was a lot of heartache and literally, grief.

Albert Einstein said, "Life is like riding a bicycle - in order to keep your balance you must keep moving." This is so true. You and I eventually have to move along. Life is a circle. Sometimes it feels more like a circus than a circle. Nonetheless, the sun sets and the moon rises and another day begins again with or without us. How we handle these days is what matters. Who or what we put our faith in also matters. First and foremost there are no 'shoulds', only suggestions. Take what you like and leave the rest.

As for the question: What do *you* want? You may not even know at this point. I will say this, memories are great and they can keep us going, for awhile. However, if you allow them to take over your life you have no room for your dreams. I have prayed for Vision. Yes vision, and no, not eyesight! Vision produces discipline. I found I had to say no to outside things. Just doing things for the sake of keeping busy is not the same as dealing with grief. Being busy will not get you through the grief process any faster, if anything, it will slow you down. You can be so busy with frivolous outside energy sapping activity that you won't have time to deal with the grief, so you won't. It's hard to think of having a dream or dreams of your own especially when you have shared a life with someone and you had dreams together. It's very hard.

There will come a day when you will choose to live life again. You will have to make choices on your own. We all will. It is very difficult to lose the person in our lives that was the one person that seemed to validate our very existence on a daily basis. Who is going to validate your dreams now? Who will support you emotionally now? Who will be there for you? These are tough questions, but they have answers.

I was talking with my sister Kathy after Jack was gone about six months. I was saying that I had truly lost the one person who validated my existence in the world. Her response was, "*One* of the people who validated your existence in the world." It took me back for a second. She was right; I understood what she was saying. There are always more people than we think that validate who we are. She knew what I meant; I was talking about on a daily basis. I also knew what she meant; that I was not alone. And neither are you. We may *feel* alone, and like no one really understands what we're going through or have gone through. That may be true. They may not have lost someone dear to them yet, but they will. We all do. Pastor Myron Prok once said to me, "No one gets through this life unscathed." He was right. People who haven't been devastated by grief don't understand the depth of emotions and the feelings, the confusing highs and lows of it all. It has been my experience that even if they have not, they try to understand it. People try to support us the best they can. If they have not yet experienced a great loss we cannot expect them to understand, that would be unfair on our part. They have no idea what's going on inside our heads. It's up to us to share it so that they can help us. People aren't mind readers. They don't know what they don't know. If we don't let them in, even in a very small way, how can we expect them to know how to reach out to us?

After all, this illness, or loss, that you are grieving, may be about someone else but it certainly affects you and your peace of mind. We all have a part in it. We often don't know where the boundaries are, or maybe we don't know where they should be, or even *if* they should be. I can tell you that yes, there should be some boundaries. Boundaries are necessary for your own sanity. If you don't set some boundaries the lines blur and you are off in another world and you will find yourself exhausted, angry, frightened, and unable to comprehend what the heck is going on around you.

So, what do you want for yourself? It's a tough question. You may not even remember what your favorite color is by now. I was asked that question. What was my favorite color and I had to think for a few seconds before I answered it. You may have been so focused, as I was, on what was going on around me that I had no idea of who I was anymore. I didn't know what I wanted. I didn't know what I liked to do on my own. I was never on my own before so how would I know?

What I knew I wanted was to move from Cleveland to Seattle near my daughter, my son-in-law and grandchildren. That was part of Plan B. I did that and am grateful to be so close now. I also wanted to give up Nursing and work on a horse farm with horses and buy a horse. Okay, so the whole working on a horse farm and buying a horse hasn't worked out…..yet! It's still on the top of my list. I have the boots but not the horse! I did work with someone taking riding lessons and almost bought a horse, but decided against that particular one. My second option is to do volunteer work with at-risk teens working with horses. That I can do.

I had to find out what I *could* do, what I wanted to do, and not worry about what I wasn't able to do right away. I had options presented to me and I followed up on them. I also wanted to get this book finished. That too was on the top of my list for two reasons: 1.) I want to support the Village Project and 2.) It's been very therapeutic for me to write this. Journaling and writing have always been therapeutic for me. Do what you can to put something on your list that you want to do and then do it. It doesn't have to be something like writing a book. I started this book some time ago when Jack was diagnosed the second time. What I put on my list was to *finish* it. If what you always wanted to do was take an Art class, then take one. Check it out and see how you like it. I have a friend, Vicky, who decided to take an Interior Design class. She wanted to take the class to see if she might want to change her career. She loves it! You don't have to get a four year degree to find out if you like something or not. Just take one class and try it out. Nothing ventured, nothing gained.

I have gotten out of my comfort zone and made new friends. I had left Cleveland shortly after Jack died and moved to the Seattle area. It was difficult at first but I made myself find some new friends. I had a lot of friends in Cleveland, but that wasn't helping me out here! Somehow Facebook doesn't do it for me. I need to connect with people personally. Anyway, I have met a group of women that I like and we have breakfast with occasionally on Saturday morning and we also go on long weekend trips that are not too far from home. We rented a house at a resort for a weekend and a group of us shared the cost. We had a lot of fun! I didn't think fun would be in the picture for me anymore, but it was, and it is. I just had to be willing to get out there and make myself meet some people. Church is also a good place to meet some people. I have met some people at church and got involved for a while feeding the homeless. It was a humbling experience. I felt like I was contributing instead of worrying about me. All I have to do is really look around and I will see pretty quickly where there may be a need I can fill or help fill, close to home.

Sometimes I get scared and think I won't have enough saved for retirement. After all, the more you read about it the costlier it gets! So, I decided to save what I could and still live my life with my dreams intact. There's no reason that I can't. I don't plan on retiring any time soon so to fret about it makes no sense whatsoever to me. I have five grandchildren that I adore that live not twenty minutes from me. I have a good job, a great place to live and the rest will fall into place.

None of this has been an easy thing to do. At times it may look like I have it all together, but that's not how it is. It was hard to put myself out there and make new friends. Trying to find a church that fit my needs was also hard. It's like church shopping for lack of a better term.

Financially it has been difficult. When Jack and I decided to sell our home it was due to the financial stress of medical bills. We decided to downsize. For a time it was working. Then we had to downsize a second time. By the third time Jack had been through four major surgeries in five years, and we downsized again. Only this time we had to go into Bankruptcy because we were unable to pay all of the medical bills. It was devastating for both of us. We did the Bankruptcy where you pay it back over a period of time. It was a lot of money taken from my paycheck every month, but we felt it necessary to pay it back. No one goes through these types of illnesses and surgeries without financial consequences. My saving grace was that Jack was still here then. This is when I wished we had more life insurance on him. We had a small amount, but not nearly enough to put a dent in the financial mess we were in. He was uninsurable from that standpoint so we could not increase the amount. I know it bothered Jack tremendously, and myself as well, but we did what we could and hoped we would come out of it all okay.

Jack died and I did not come out of it okay at first. I, like a lot of single people make it paycheck to paycheck. I try to look at the positive things in my life every day. There are things like my family and friends that you cannot put a price on. In that sense I am a rich woman. Eventually the financial piece will work itself out. I won't be the only one working past Retirement age.

The more difficult piece is trying to put a life together on your own. Moving across the country is one thing. Having to make every other major decision can be daunting. I had to find a place to live. I had to decide if I liked it, not if *we* liked it. There was no 'we'. I had car payments that still had to be made and paid bills that had to be paid. I had to use my budget from Plan B. It gave me an idea of what I would need to live on. I will say this; I needed more money to live on than I had planned on in my budget from Plan B. It will all work out in the end. I have never been on the street, and I am far from that. I have to remind myself that wants and needs are two different things.

Going to the grocery store was difficult at first. I found myself standing in the aisle wondering if I should get something we both liked. Then in a flash I realized that I was the only one. That was hard. I had tears in my eyes a lot in the grocery store. I didn't even know what I liked. I would pick up things that Jack used to like and I didn't particularly, and had to put it back on the shelf. I had, and still have a really hard time cooking for one. I just try to eat more fruits, yogurt and sandwiches. Cooking for one is not my thing. If the truth be known, cooking for two wasn't my thing either. Jack grilled a lot, and my idea of cooking is putting a potato in the microwave. Good thing Jack didn't mind. He would just pick up his dinner on the way home from Heinen's (a great grocery store in Bay Village) and he was happy as a clam. For me? Well, Cheerios will do for dinner. Okay, Fruit Loops too!

Going out to the movie by myself at first felt weird. I have found that it's actually a little fun after all. I can go with a friend, or I can go and watch the movie myself without anyone chatting through it. Either way works for me now. I just had to do it. Granted, doing some things alone is not fun. Going to the Pumpkin Patch with grandchildren is certainly more fun than going alone and just wandering through and buying a pumpkin! I do find myself sometimes thinking about what Jack is missing with the grandchildren. It bothers me that we aren't doing things together with them. But I am sure if he could have he certainly would have.

When It's All Said
And Done

"There are only ways to live your life. One is as though nothing is a miracle. The other is as though everything is a miracle" said Albert Einstein. Jack was one of the biggest miracles in my life. I don't say that lightly. I have not always believed in miracles. I believe everything happens for a reason. Life itself is a miracle, regardless of how long we are here to live it. We speak of people having untimely deaths. I'm not sure there is an untimely death. People may leave us sooner than we want, sometimes much sooner. I believe people are in our lives for a reason, a season or a lifetime. Jack was in mine for almost thirty years, twenty six of them married. He was here for many reasons, many seasons, and one great lifetime.

This will be by far the hardest journey you will take, as have we. I say we because Jack and I were in this together. I am guessing you also are on this journey with someone, or have been through this with someone. No one can do this alone. It's not possible. We are not shatterproof; we need people to help hold us together when we can't. The grief journey has been a difficult one for me. My suggestion is you don't do it alone. I will talk more about that later.

I am a Registered Nurse, which in no way makes me an expert on life limiting diseases or death. I have, however, seen my fair share of both. For several years I worked with hospice patients. I learned a lot from them. I also learned when my husband was diagnosed that I would not, and could not, be the Hospice Nurse for him. I needed to be his wife. I needed to be the supportive one, not the one giving directions. Although it was great to have the experience of hospice behind me, I knew I simply needed to be the wife. I did ask a lot of questions of doctors and nurses. Habit I guess. Sometimes I was uncomfortable with the answers. I knew how to read his chart and look for clues as to what was going on. Sometimes too much information isn't a good thing. Jack didn't want a lot of information; I on the other hand did. I wanted the answers, the labs, and the reports. I wanted it all. I suppose I thought there would be some measure of control in having that information rolling around in my head. There was not.

When it's all said and done I needed to remember that it's never really all said and done. There will always be reminders. There will always be birthday and anniversary dates, Mother's Day and Father's Day, Grandparents Day. The list can seem almost endless. There will be holidays and graduations without them. It can be tough. It is tough. There are also ways to work through it.

For me, when it came to my Dad, who died when I was nineteen of lung cancer, I honor his birthday every year with a birthday card. I specifically pick out one that I would send him if he were here. I write a note in it and tell him what's going on in my life at the time. It may seem odd, but to me it's very therapeutic. I write about his grandchildren and now his great-grandchildren. He's been gone a long time. It doesn't matter; he is still here in my heart. Memories of the heart do not fade with time. I do the same at Christmas. I take the cards to a special place, either the woods or near a lake, somewhere I sense my dad would have liked. I drop them off and I leave. I don't go back to see if they're still there. It's the writing and leaving of the message that's important to me. I'm not concerned if anyone reads it. I don't make it so that anyone really knows who it goes to or came from. I simply write on the envelope: Dad and sign it Kerry. Okay, so now if you find a card in the woods with my name on it you may have guessed I put it there. It's okay to read it. I went back only once a few years ago on Thanksgiving. I put a card in the woods near our home and then for some reason went back to see if it was there. It was, but it had been opened and someone read the note inside. They did, however, prop it back up against the birch tree that I set it against. They respected it enough to do that.

I recall many years ago that I was in the mall picking up a watch battery for Jack. I kept ending up in this particular jewelry store. I wasn't going to a jewelry store, I was going to a kiosk in the center of the mall. I circled around again, and again I ended up in the same jewelry store. I thought to myself that it was pretty odd but that I was going to go with it and see what happened.

"Can I help you?" the Saleswoman said politely smiling

"Yes.." I hesitated "I need a gift."

"Ok, what kind of gift?"

I had no idea and I had no idea for whom I was in there for! I waited a second and the words fell out of my mouth.

"For a little girl"

"And how old is this little girl?"

"Six. She's six and she's very special." Oh man! Now what!? Words were coming out of my mouth and I'm buying a present in a jewelry store for a six year old and I have no idea who she is let alone why I'm doing this!

"Do you have an idea of what she likes?"

"Um, I'm not really sure." What an understatement. At this point I decided to just go with it.

"Alright, would you like to look at a charm bracelet or a necklace?" she glanced at me with questioning eyes.

"A necklace. I need a necklace with a charm on it. I want a chain that's never going to break." I felt myself getting a little excited about this whole thing, still unaware as to why I was really doing this.

"Well, we have quite a collection of small gold charms here. Some are on sale and"

"I'm not worried about the price." I cut her off. Really? I'm not worried about the price?

"Okay, let's look at these" she smiled. I'd smile too if someone came into my jewelry store and said they weren't worried about the price.

I settled on a small gold kitten with a ball. "I'll take this one. And I want it on a really good quality chain."

"We have some very nice gold chains on sale right now," she looked up.

"I'm not worried about the price; I want a really good chain that's never going to break."

"Okay then, I have a solid gold rope chain with a double clasp."

"That's it. I'll take it. Please gift wrap this for me."

"She must be one special little girl to spend this kind of money on" she smiled.

"She is, and she's so worth it!" I smiled, "You have no idea" I said as I took my little package and left.

I knew when I looked at the charms what I was doing in that store. You see, it was close to Father's Day and Jack and I were going to Pittsburgh to find my dad's grave. I had not been there since I was nineteen. I realized in the store that I had never in my life been able to buy my dad a Father's Day gift. I trusted my instinct and went with it. I was drawn to the store, I picked out the gift, and it was a gift for my dad that I would wear this necklace often and never forget him. Yes, it was an interesting way to go about it, but that didn't matter to me. What mattered was I followed my instinct. It's what my sister Kathy calls a God Wink. A blessing that seems to come from nowhere. It was a blessing that calmed my soul when it came to my Dad.

In July Jack and I found our way to Allegheny Cemetery in Pittsburgh and to my dad's grave. I set the necklace on the grave, which to that point I had not worn yet. I said a prayer and had Jack put it on me. I left his Father's Day card on the grave before we left. It felt complete. Unless you have lost a parent you may not quite understand this yet. It was my way of saying, "Dad, you're still in the memory of my heart every day." That took place many years ago and every time I put on that necklace, which is often, and on the same chain I said had to be strong enough to never break, I smile.

On what would have been my dad's eightieth birthday I had mailed a card to a friend and asked her to place it somewhere special in the Cleveland MetroParks. I had moved from the Cleveland area to Seattle but the MetroParks have always been special to me growing up. Patty did that, and she did something more. She called me and said, "Dad's card was delivered and I sang Happy Birthday to him!" Tears instantly came to my eyes; she understood how much it meant to me. She got it. Some people will. We just need to ask those people for help when we need it. Patty was with me when I went through the death of my younger brother, and with Jack. She is one of a handful of people I can call anytime day or night and she will be there. She has been there. Rini is another one. Rini was with me through Jack's surgeries, chemotherapy, cardiac rehab, and just about everything in between. If you have friends like these you are blessed. They are truly god with skin on. They are the angels among us that get us through.

There are many ways to honor a person who is no longer with us, this was just one way I found helpful to me.

When I left Cleveland I left with a lot of great memories. Often time's grief tried to enter my thoughts and replace them with negative ones. I had to guard against that. I don't want to forget all of the great memories we had. My life with Jack was a huge part of my life. The first Christmas without him was very difficult. I didn't save the small tree we loved to decorate, but I did save the small ornaments. Christmas ornaments are memories on branches. Those memories are important. I bought a new tree and had my grandson Anderson help me decorate it. I did not give up on Christmas, I just knew it would be totally different, and it was. I was in a new place, alone with my tree and not much under it because all the grandkids gifts were at my daughter's home. I felt homeless in my heart. I had a place to go, and I did go there, but my heart felt empty for the most part. Holidays are tough to get through when you're not suffering a loss let alone when you are. Tears fell, and I prayed a lot. I needed to focus on what was still good in my life and that was being with family for me. I was with family, and I did the best I could to be cheerful. It went okay. Grief needs distractions sometimes, and maybe just making Christmas cookies can be that distraction.

Life is better by choice than chance. We may not always get a chance to do what we want to in life but we get a choice to do what we are doing at the moment. We have a choice of attitudes, reactions and who is in our circle of friends who can support us. We have a choice of healthy relationships which support us or unhealthy relationships which drag us down. We will often have the chance to reevaluate our lives. A chance to refocus on what's important now. Yes, we may not know what to do for some time, and that's okay. When you have the chance to look at it and you are able to make some changes you will.

When I look back through the things I have gone through in my life and with Jack, I can only say that the fingerprints of God are all over it. I may not have recognized it at the time, but I clearly saw it when I took some time to look at what I went through. My prayer is that you find the grace in your own religion or faith that helps you find your way. I believe that everything runs through the hands of God. I had to acknowledge where I was and learn to live one day at a time, often one hour at a time to get through my grief. Is it over for me now? Not at all. I still have tears and they have cleansed my soul at times. Sometimes they have not. It depends on what triggers them. For the first year the 30th of every month was a reminder to me that Jack died on the 30th of the month of April. Now the months go by and it's not as striking to me as it was at first. Sometimes the month ends and I don't think of it at all. Yes, this may sound like a little thing here, but it's not. The anniversary of a death is significant.

I went to Cleveland on the first anniversary of Jack's death to visit his grave. My sister Kathy drove down from New York to meet me there. We went to the cemetery and she wandered off so that I could be alone with my thoughts. I sat down on the grass for a few minutes and talked with Jack. I have always been able to sense his spirit around me. I didn't feel it there. It was odd. I felt out of place being there, like nothing was there for me. I knew instinctively that Jack's spirit was not there. I said, "Jack, you're not here. I came all this way to be with you and you aren't even here. We're going to lunch!" I laughed out loud. He would have loved it! It was his sense of humor. Kathy and I went to lunch and we talked about it. I said I felt he wasn't there with me. She understood that. You may too.

My niece Tara had said to me when she called me after Jack died, "He's been restored." I just agreed with her but I really didn't dwell on it too much. I remember saying to my sister, "So, what the heck does that mean?!" She said, "I really don't know." During the funeral service it was mentioned that Jack was restored. Again I'm hearing something I have no clue about really. I will tell you what happened some months later. I was in my room, upset about my situation in life as it were, and crying. I was getting angry and I could feel it welling up inside me. I said, "Jack! I don't even know where you are! Are you here? Are you in heaven? I don't know what to do or think anymore." Later that night I went to bed. I was tired and crying and fell asleep. Just before I woke up, I was half awake and felt like I was in a dreamlike state. I opened my eyes and Jack's presence was there. I swear to this. I looked at him, and he said nothing. I saw that he was wearing his favorite jeans and a long-sleeved light blue T-shirt. I looked at his face and he smiled at me and winked. His eyes were clear, his skin was clear. He looked like he had before he was ever touched by cancer. He looked young and vibrant, like he did fourteen years before. I remember smiling and he was gone. I felt like I knew he was okay now. He *had* been restored as it were. I don't know if you believe this or not, and that's okay. I believe the world is a very spiritual place. I believe that Angels protect us and sometimes our loved ones are or have been those Angels for us.

I have tried to take care of myself the best way I can. I can take care of my own needs. I can nourish myself in the right way. I can try to heal the broken places in my soul. I can determine what is right and wrong for me. I am more patient than I was before. The world is a safe place for me to live in, and I can create positive memories for myself from now on. I know that I am supported in many ways. I have accepted the reality of this death and its consequences. I have felt the pain of the loss, when it was fresh, and after some time. I have had to search for meaning in my own life. I struggled with wanting to even live this life anymore. All of these things resolved over time, not overnight. I had to reconcile a lot of things in my own mind and it took time. I will continue to do so, as I'm sure things will come up again and I will again face it and deal with it the best I can. And so will you.

If someone were to ask me if there was anything I would have done differently I would have to say no. We all do what we are capable of doing at any given time. Going through an illness or death is no different. To go back and reflect on what I could have, or should have done differently makes no sense. It would only add to my grief. There are no 'do over's' with death. I loved Jack with my whole heart. If I could have done something differently then I would have. But this is how my life unfolded with Jack, and I wouldn't have it any other way. Yes, I miss him and would have wanted to spend the rest of my life with him, but that's not what happened. The reality is that he is gone and I am here.

I would like to close this book with a poem by George R. Monseur that Jack asked to be read at his funeral:

MISS ME BUT LET ME GO

*When I come to the end of the road and the
sun has set for me,*
*I want no rites in a gloom filled room, why cry
for a soul set free?*
*Miss me a little......but not too long. And not
with your head bowed low.*
*Remember the love that once was shared,
miss me... but then let me go.*
*For this is a journey we all must take and
each must go alone.*
*It's all part of the Master's plan, a step on the
road to home.*
*When you are lonely and sick of heart go to
the friends we know,*
And bury your sorrows in doing good deeds.
                Miss me ... but let me go.

With gratitude and grace I wish you peace in your
heart and Soul – Kerry

Printed in the United States
By Bookmasters